Ski Technique and Instruction Manual

Book 1 — Basic Ski System

The Official teaching manual of the
British Association of Ski Instructors

Revised 4th Edition

EDITOR : DOUG GODLINGTON

Member of the International
Ski Instructors Association

i

© BASI 1985

ISBN 0 904212 00 9

First British Edition published 1973
Revised published 1978
Revised published 1983
Revised published 1985

Published and distributed by Secretary of BASI, Inverdruie, Aviemore PH22 1QH

CONTENTS

FOREWORD

The revision and reprint of this 3rd issue of the BASI Manual reflects the Association's continued growth in the field of Ski Instruction. Development of technique and teaching methods undergo constant review. In this context, the Second BASI Manual will cover further technical aspects of coaching skiing. However, this original issue of the Basic Technique is still a valuable cornerstone in the programme of BASI's work.

With no outside financial aid, BASI has been represented at the Interski Congresses in Zao, Japan 1979 and Sesto, Italy 1983. The honour to be invited to present a Demonstration Team at the congresses, is proudly undertaken by BASI. This role internationally, small though it may be, is very important — ISIA meetings and Interski Congresses are the world's pulse on future developments in Technique and Instruction. As a duty to their members BASI will ensure that they will continue to be represented.

It is a long way back to the first BAPSI Course in 1963 with lots of changes in this time, many members have gone different ways — worldwide. One member however, who has steered BASI through this time as the Chairman, was honoured to be our first President — Jack Thomson, long may his skis slide — many thanks, Jack!

As this issue goes to press, the Technical Committee and Technical Director with the Editor are putting together the last details for the second Manual, ready for print. One of the jobs that is undertaken behind the scenes involved in BASI's work. In this respect, the services of the BASI Secretary continues to be invaluable and appreciated, increasingly so with the expansion of Technical Publications and the new training and assessment programmes for the future.

Doug Godlington.

1

HISTORY OF SKIING

**Development of Ski Technique —
Ski Instruction in Britain**

**Development of
Ski Technique**

There is no doubt that skiing in a very rudimentary form, began many centuries ago.

The Hoting skis dug out of a peat bog in Sweden, and other ancient skis found in Finland, date back over 2000 B.C.

From Scandinavia through to China, history and folk-lore record many instances in the use of skis as a means of cross-country travel in winter. Design of these early skis varied from crude short, broad boards covered in fur skins, while others were of one long and one short ski — using a push off the short ski to glide forward on the longer one.

Illustrated records of Norwegian and Swedish armies equipped with skis go back to 1200, with stories of heroism, such as the rescue of the infant King Hakon and many other military actions through the centuries. It was for the correct use of skis that the first Ski Instruction Guide was issued to Norwegian soldiers in 1765.

While there is no record of skiing in the Alps during this period, it is to another enterprising Norwegian that modern skiing owes much of its origins. Sondre Norheim, from Moredal in the Telemark district made skis of a similar design to those used today. His skis were waisted in the centre and enabled the first curved turns to be performed, while the bindings were made to fix the boots firmly to the skis.

Fridtjoff Nansen's published account of crossing Greenland, with its exciting detailed description of this skiing expedition in 1888, fired the imagination of many people to take up skiing as a sport. The great exploration period of the 19th Century saw the increased use of skis. Characters like 'Snowshoe' Thomson used 12ft long skis to carry the miners' mail across the Californian Sierra Nevada for 20 years !

Ski Clubs were formed, jumping hills were built, with competitions for jumping, cross-country and slalom racing. Skiing as a sport had arrived — a mere 4,000 years after the first skiers !

**1860 — Telemark and
Christiania Turns**

With the skis he designed, Sondre Norheim was able to perform long sweeping turns — the Telemark — named after his home district. He further developed the first parallel swings — the Christiania — named after the district now called Oslo.

The elegant Telemark with its long leg spread, and still used by cross-country skiers, was used to steer the skis through deep snow without losing too much speed.

This technique was to form the basis of skiing that spread throughout Europe and North America from 1880 into the 1900's.

1890 — Snowplough and Stem Turns

Alpine slopes with its steeper terrain brought an extra problem to these early ski pioneers. Mathias Zdarsky of Lillienfield, Austria, using shorter skis and metal bindings, developed the Snowplough and stemming to make slow controlled turns, although still using one long pole to brake with. In 1896 he published in detail, 'Alpine Lillienfelder Skifahrtechnik', that was to provide the basis of alpine ski technique.

1900 — Ski Schools

From the early 1900's the sport became established as a winter recreation holiday. Ski Schools became part of the scene, with the followers of the two systems — Nordic and Alpine — laying claim that each respective system was the better method of skiing. An Englishman, Vivian Caulfield, blended the two systems together, eliminating the one pole method. In his book 'How to Ski' published in 1910, he revealed and explained the elements of skiing mechanics. The Richardson Brothers introduced Ski Tests at Davos.

1910 — Stem Christiania

In the Austrian Arlberg, Hannes Schneider refined the stem and Telemark to produce the Stem Christiania in 1909. Colonel Bilgeri and others analysed ski instruction still further, until Schneider with his emphasised up and down body movements, had made famous the 'Arlberg Technique' of the 1920's.

1920 — Slalom Racing

During this period Sir Arnold Lunn worked untiringly to revolutionise competitive skiing. He devised the modern form of Slalom racing, and this in turn was to play an important part in the further development of ski technique. The Federation International de Ski (FIS) was founded in 1924.

1930 — Rotation and Parallel Skiing

In the 1930's skis and bindings underwent further design changes, and with the invention of steel edges by Rudolph Lettner, it was possible to have better edge control.

The French with Emile Allais, his Ski School at Chamonix, emphasised the learning of Parallel turns using a rotation of the upper body, through a progression of side-slipping and uphill swings.

1950 — Wedeln, Short Swings, and Christiania Leger

Until the 1950's ski technique remained static, before a new phase began of national identities claiming the merits of a country's particular technique and teaching system.

The Austrians, with a State-backed ski teaching industry under the direction of Prof. Stefan Kruckenhauser, developed a system with 'Wedeln' as the goal, and 'Reverse Shoulder' as a key to the learning progression. The Swiss too, worked out a system into Short Swings using more slide-slipping and less extreme body positions. Meanwhile the French, in their efforts to produce natural skiing movements, modified the rotation parallel turn into the 'light Christiania Turn', using 'projection cirulaire' with subtle unweighting body movements. This still forms part of the French ski technique system.

1960 — Interski and Unification of Ski Technique

With the expansion of skiing as a holiday sport, the general pattern over the world was to a more unified ski technique. Excessive body angulation had been replaced by the importance of leg movements in the Austrian system. All basic ski technique systems have had unnecessary steps removed to bring pupils into parallel skiing earlier. The Americans, through the Professional Ski Instructors Association, produced a national technique using natural positions and total motion to give fluent skiing, in 1964.

Interski Congresses every four years give demonstrations and talks in the common interest for technique development.

1970 — Compression Turns and advanced parallel skiing. Free style skiing

Changes in equipment design — short skis, moulded boots — together with racing technology, have played an important part in the continued development in ski instruction methods. Terrain technique and advanced parallel manoeuvres have brought new words into ski language — Compression Turns, Avalement,

Jet Turns, Step Turns — using lower body position, signifying another new phase in the evolution of ski technique.
Skiing in a more art-form showed itself on the slopes. Free-style skiing competitions for Ballet, Aerial and mogul-bashing were organised — yet another outlet to test the outer limits of ski technique.

British Ski Instruction Development

In 1962 the British Association of Professional Ski Instructors (BAPSI) was founded as the controlling body for training and grading ski instructors. The opening up of the snows in the Scottish Highlands during the early 1960's, with lift-served runs and organised skiing holidays, saw the need to establish a responsible body for technique and teaching standards. This was the beginning of the work by the Association for training courses, and members throughout the United Kingdom and abroad. Instruction had been given much earlier on Scottish snows. In 1948 a ski school was run by Bill Bracken and Patsy Richardson, from Newtonmore, more as a break from their alpine club activities. However the Scottish Council of Physical Recreation centre at Glenmore had already included skiing courses in their programme of outdoor activities. But it was not until into the 1950's that commercial ski instruction arrived on the scene. The village of Carrbridge saw organised Ski Schools with Austrian Ski Instructors. Other Hoteliers set up ski instruction service with both British and Continental teachers, as the prospects of winter sports holidays became a reality.

By 1962, Cairngorm, Glencoe and Glenshee were developed ski areas, offering organised ski instruction to skiers, as part of the service to the winter tourist industry. The standard of this service was required to be administered, and accordingly the Scottish Tourist Board, S.C.P.R. together with Ski Schools, formed BAPSI to carry out this work.

The Association was invited to become a member of the International Ski Instructors Association in 1964, and have sent delegates and demonstration teams to technical meetings and congresses, in this way keeping abreast of current international developments in techniques and teaching methods.

With the formal recognition of BASI (Professional now deleted from the title) by the National Ski Federation, under its Ski Instruction Council, BASI has an important role covering all aspects of instruction in Britain, whether on snow or artificial slopes. Instructor Courses are now held in the Alps as well as home snows, with BASI providing trainers for Ski Party Leader and artificial ski slope coaching courses.

An Instruction Film on the BASI Technique has been produced, and this is part of the future projects and policies that the Association have in mind both for its membership and instruction in general.

The publication of the first Instruction Manual made a significant contribution to BASI's role in British skiing, and it is hoped that this revised edition will continue in this work.

2

SKI TECHNIQUE & BASIC TEACHING SYSTEM

BASIC SKIING TECHNIQUE

Basic skiing introduces the beginner to the sport, progressing through to parallel turns.

These progressive steps in technique give the learner skier the fundamentals of skiing control — balance and basic turning movements. Once these fundamentals have been acquired the skier is mobile and able to use ski lifts. With practice running using lifts, together with correct instruction, the turning movements can be continuously linked to obtain a feeling of rhythm. The aim is to develop these basic turning movements so that the student learns quickly the essentials for parallel skiing.

The standard progression into Parallel turns, highlights certain steps such as the Basic Swing. However, in practice some skiers learn more quickly while others find it more difficult to acquire the technique. To cover these possibilities there are alternatives to the standard progression while still retaining the main essentials of the basic parallel turn.

The novice skier who is able to hold a good basic stance over the skis, and achieve a feeling of turning the skis with the legs and feet, is then competent to ski down most general skiing terrain. A good grounding in the essentials for skiing in control, will give the learner confidence to enjoy skiing and lead to an interest to develop their technique further.

Teaching Plan — Basic Skiing

As in the first edition of the manual, each Technique stage has been accompanied by a description of the complementary teaching method required. To help the candidate Instructor and the student skier, the Teaching Method has been amplified. All the information necessary is given to teach a particular manoeuvre in practice, or as required on a Course Teaching Assessment.

The overall Teaching Plan for basic skiing advises the Instructor which methods to teach and apply the progression of the various manoeuvres, with the important points to stress as each stage is reached. At the same time, the Instructor must be flexible in his or her application of the Teaching Plan — there is no hard and fast rule to stick rigidly to the progression. According to the student's ability, snow conditions etc., be ready to adapt the teaching method with the aim of leading them as soon as possible into parallel skiing.

Choosing the **correct terrain** in teaching the elementary steps, makes all the difference between putting off or frightening a pupil to progress quickly into skiing easy downhill runs.

Exercises and Aids are used to separate the various manoeuvres into specific parts, refining or correcting the student's technique as necessary. The suggested exercises are for helping the student acquire balance and control correctly, as well as directly breaking down the final manoeuvre into several parts. However, the Instructor should be prepared to create additional exercises which will help the student to become proficient without losing interest.

Common Faults are outlined as an essential part of understanding the basic technique and application of the teaching method.

Aids such as the use of short skis, an open stance, skiing round slalom poles, group skiing, games, or any other innovations should be encouraged to help the student, as well as give variety to the skiing sessions.

Book 1

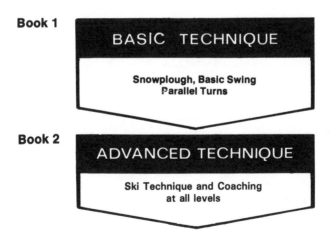

BASIC TECHNIQUE

**Snowplough, Basic Swing
Parallel Turns**

Book 2

ADVANCED TECHNIQUE

**Ski Technique and Coaching
at all levels**

PROGRESSION INTO PARALLEL TURNS

All pupils learning to ski are not equally proficient, therefore the progression into Parallel skiing is divided into alternative methods.

STANDARD METHOD

The **Standard Method** covers the majority of novice skiers, where the Snowplough is gradually phased out through the Basic Swing into Basic Parallel Turns.

DIRECT METHOD

For skiers who are quicker to learn and are able to turn the skis in close linked movements down the fall-line the **Direct Method** is outlined.

FAN METHOD

For skiers who find it difficult to eliminate stemming, the **Fan Method** is suggested as a way of progressing into Parallel skiing.

All of these methods lead finally into the overall plan of teaching the student to link the turns closer together in the form of Short Swings. The skier has then acquired the basic skills necessary to accomplish most downhill ski-runs safely.

BASIC TEACHING SYSTEM

Section 1 — Basic Skiing

Introduction to Skis

Walking & Climbing Steps

Straight Running

Snowplough

Turns

Section 4 — Fan Method

Traverse

Side Slip

Swing to the Hill

Basic Parallel Turns
by progressive steeper
Swings to the Hill

Section 3—Direct Method

Snowplough

Wedel

Short Turns
in fall-line

Narrow Plough

Rhythm

Basic Parallel Turns

Section 2 — Basic Swing

Traverse

Side Slip

Swing to the Hill

Basic Swing

Basic Parallel Turns

Section 5—Parallel Turns

Use of Planted Stick

Linked
Parallel Turns

Section 6

Parallel
Short Swings

Section 7

Compression
Turns

SECTION 1 —
INTRODUCTION TO THE USE OF SKIS

Beginners find skis awkward to carry and at first to wear. It is necessary therefore, to become familiar with the correct way of carrying and the limitations that they impose on your movements when in use. In the interests of safety, it is important to be able to check and adjust the ski bindings as well as ensure that they are fitted with some form of brake or retaining device, should the ski become detached from your boot.

Carrying Skis

Fasten the skis together with the soles facing inwards, and balance the mid-section on the shoulder, with the tips held forward. For safety hold the forward part of the skis down, ensuring that the rear part of the skis do not hit other skiers or obstacles etc. Carry the ski sticks in the free hand and use them for support as you walk. In crowded confined areas carry the skis tips up, with the arm held around the skis, gripping them at the mid section.

Putting on skis

Preferably choose a smooth flat area, and place the skis parallel on the snow — about 6″ apart. Place the ski sticks on either side of the skis so that they can be used for support. Clean off snow from the boot soles — scraping off across the steel edge of an upturned ski is one method of clearing the boot sole.

Fix the boot toe and heel squarely into the bindings, and secure the retaining straps or clips.

When putting skis on when standing across a slope, it is important to lay the skis horizontally to the slope. It is easier to fix the lower ski on first, stamping out a platform on which to stand and then fasten on the upper ski.

Ski Stick Grip

The stick handle is held by passing the hand upwards through the strap — gripping both strap and handle in the palm of the hand.

INTRODUCTION TO USE OF SKIS

Carrying Skis

Putting Skis On

Ski Stick Grip

Walking and Climbing Steps

WALKING AND CLIMBING STEPS

Getting used to the feeling of wearing skis is essential for the learner skier. Start with stationary exercises on the spot, lifting, sliding and stepping one ski at at time, to become accustomed to the limit of movement imposed on the skier when wearing skis and boots.

Walking and Gliding Step

Slide the skis forward by using a normal walking stride — push the knee towards the tip with each stride, without lifting the skis off the snow. Track the skis comfortably apart with each sliding step. As each ski slides forward, the opposite arm and stick are swung naturally forward and angled to give forward push. The movement is a continuous rhythmic sliding motion of legs and skis together with the opposing arm and stick plant to give a push and glide.

Gliding forward with both skis together is made by reaching forward with both arms, planting the sticks forward of the boots by a strong downward push and follow through rearwards, to lean well forward into the glide.

Star Turn

To turn round when stationary, open out the tips or heels of the skis. Stepping the legs sideways. Use the sticks for support while stepping round.

Falling and Getting Up

Falling down is part of the process of learning to ski — allow the legs to relax and fold to drop the seat in the snow at the side. Extend the legs on hitting the snow to avoid the knees digging into the snow, lie fully stretched out if possible. Try to avoid reaching down with the hand extended into the snow to arrest the fall.

To stand up again — first sit on the uphill side of the skis parallel and across the slope. From the sitting position on the uphill side, push off with the hands and sticks close in to the body, leaning well forward over the boots to regain a standing position.

CLIMBING STEPS

Side Step

To climb directly up the slope, the skis are stepped horizontally. The uphill edges of the skis are set into the snow, by bending the knees forwards and sideways towards the slope. Lift and step the uphill ski into the snow, reaching uphill to plant the stick at the same time. The lower ski is stepped up parallel and firmly set alongside, stepping up the slope with support from the sticks, and ensuring that the skis are held across the slope.

Diagonal Side Step

Climbing diagonally across the slope, the skis are stepped up and forwards, ensuring the uphill edges are set into the snow. The sticks are used as support with each stepping action.

Herringbone Step

On gentle slopes, the skier climbs directly up the slope. By holding the skis out at an angle from the heels, a walking-stepping action is used. Lift and step the skis alternately to press on the inside edges, pushing on the sticks planted in the snow behind the boots to prevent the skis sliding backwards.

Stepping Round on the Slope

To change direction or face directly down the fall-line, it is necessary to have correct support from the ski sticks. Change the grip on the stick handle, holding the top in the palm of the hand until the arm and stick form a straight line. Place the sticks comfortably apart at arms length on the downhill forward side of the skis. While leaning on the sticks, side step the skis round, keeping the tips between the planted sticks. The edge setting of the skis into the slope will be changed as the skis are stepped across the fall-line.

Kick Turn

From a secure stance across the slope, both sticks planted uphill, kick-up the lower ski onto its heel. Allow this ski to drop parallel with the upper ski. Transfer the standing weight to the lower ski then swing the upper ski down and alongside to complete the turn and face in the opposite direction

15

Teaching Method — Introduction to Skiing

After introduction to the group, carefully go through the checks as outlined in the Section on Teaching Practice, giving assurance to the beginner new to the sport and unfamiliar with the equipment. Show how to secure and carry skis. Explain briefly the function of skis binding operation and adjustment. Demonstrate putting on skis, then have the pupils fit their own skis on. Demonstrate holding the ski stick, and begin the static exercises to acquire the feel of skis. If necessary, check the pupil for boot fit about the ankles — loosen to allow for a forward flex. Progress into walking and gliding steps as soon as possible, all the class can practice together. Demonstrate changing direction by making small angled out steps in the snow, encourage a gliding forward of the skis in the walking movement.

Lead into Side Stepping up an easy slope, using small steps, with the importance of setting the ski edges into the snow to form a platform step. The lower leg, ankle and knee are pressed into the slope to effect the edge set. Use the Herringbone step on easy gradients only. Stepping round the slope requires good support from the sticks. Step round facing both downhill and uphill.

Terrain

Flat to gentle slope, preferably. If this is not available then introduce a walking-gliding step on a horizontal traverse, emphasising edge control to track the skis.

Exercises

Static
1. Sliding skis backwards and forwards with stick support.
2. Lift alternative skis off snow — tips, heels, swing to right and left.
3. Hop both heels off the snow — parallel and into Snowplough position.
4. Reaching down to tips, boots and reaching up above head.
5. Rolling boots over from edge to edge sideways, with knee press.
6. Sitting down in the snow and getting up again.
   Star step round turn.

Walking
7. Group walking track round poles or obstacles.
8. Relay games between class split into teams.

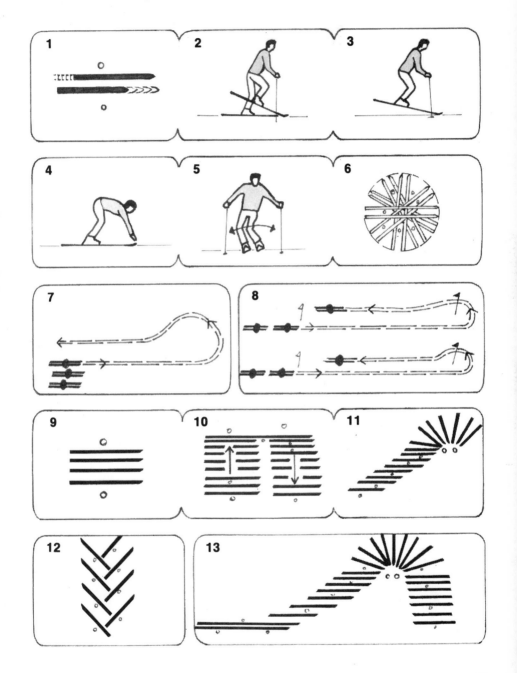

Climbing Steps

9. Side stepping between supported ski sticks.
10. Side stepping up and down the slope.
11. Side stepping diagonally and stepping round on the slope.
12. Herringbone step from the flat to slope.
13. Group track combining walking, climbing and stepping round on the slope.

Common Faults

Walking

Wrongly co-ordinated arm and leg movements — ski and arm of the same side moving forward.
Ski stick planted too far forward to give effective push.

Falling & Getting Up

Trying to push off with hand or sticks too far away from body.
Not ensuring the skis are horizontally across the slope.

Climbing Steps

Trying to step up on flat skis — without edging the skis will side slip downhill.
Not stepping the skis parallel to the line of the slope, causing them to slide off forwards or backwards.

BASIC SKIING STANCE — STRAIGHT RUNNING DOWNHILL

The Basic Stance is the relaxed position over the skis from which all turning control movements are made and is, therefore, a basis for all learning progression. Straight Running gives the beginner the first sensation of sliding directly down the slope. Teaching the learner that a good relaxed stance over the skis is essential to be able to stand up in balance.

Straight Running Stance

Skis are parallel in the fall-line, flat on the snow and comfortably hip width apart. Both skis are equally weighted, with ankles, knees and body slightly flexed. The body is now in a well balanced position over the skis. Hands are held hip high, forward away from the body. The sticks are carried parallel to the rear and clear of the snow. The head is held up, looking forward. This is the 'Open Stance' skiing position — feet hip width apart with the body flexed for stability.

Skiing through Bumps and Hollows

The legs are flexed to absorb the terrain undulations, streching into the hollows and folding the legs over the bumps.

Skating Step

The Skating Step is performed by pushing off one ski to glide onto the opposite ski.

The walking-glide movements are modified to step out successively the ski-tips at an angle to the line of direction. A strong push-off is made from each obliquely placed ski by a flex and straightening of the leg on the weighted ski. By using one or both sticks planted in the snow behind the boots, the slide forward is helped with each push off. Leaning well forward with a positive step transfer from each ski is necessary to keep the skating movements flowing.

Teaching Method — Straight Running

The Straight Running position emphasises the Basic Stance used in skiing control. Sliding downhill on selected terrain teaches the student to gain confidence in the feeling of balance control while the skis glide naturally. Exercises are demonstrated and practiced using the Open Stance tracking position for safety and stability, to enable the student to progress as quickly as possible through this stage. Step round into the fall-line, using the sticks for support, and when the skis are parallel allow them to slide forward by releasing the pressure on the sticks. Teach balance exercises first, then co-ordination exercises, followed by skiing over bumps. Introduce the skating step as a means of locomotion on flatter terrain, as an aid to help the pupil feel edge control and to be able to change direction.

Terrain

Easy gradient slope with flat runout, on prepared snow surface.

Exercises

Balance Exercises
Using wide stance, demonstrated statistically before running.
1. Knee and ankle flexing deeply.
2. Reaching down to touch boots and stand up again.
3. Sliding alternate skis forward.
4. Reaching down to pick up glove, hat, etc. from the side.
5. Bending down underneath 'hurdle gate' made from ski sticks.

Co-ordination Exercises
6. Lifting one ski heel alternately, tips on the snow.
7. Hopping both ski heels off the snow.
8. Lift and step skis to the side and back into the track.
9. Bending and stretching through bumps.
10. Stepping skis to one side progressively to change direction.

Exercises — Straight Running

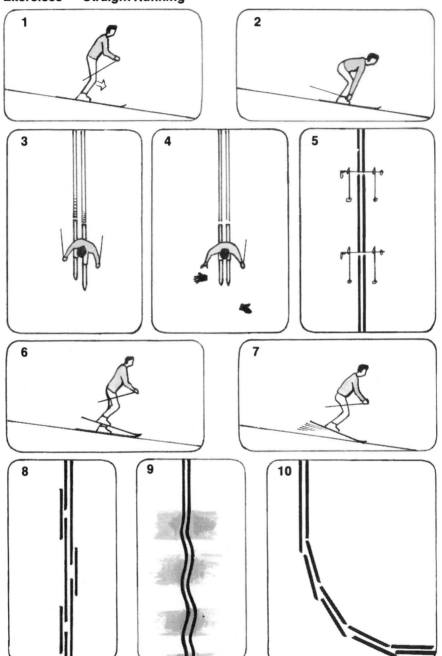

Class Activity   If there is sufficient space on the practice terrain, more than one skier can practice the exercises.

Common Faults   Stiff position over the skis. A stiff body stance results in loss of balance, or inability to track the skis correctly. The skier must be relatively relaxed to counter any influences that may affect the balance on the downhill glide — moving slightly forward over the boots to anticipate any increase in skiing speed such as when the slope steepens. If the slope flattens out then the skier should move slightly back on the heels to counter the slowing down effect.

Looking down at the skis is a natural error — a reaaction to see what is happening to the skis, but cramps the position over the skis. The head must be held up in order to look forward and anticipate the snow or any hazards ahead.

Straight Running Down Fall-line

Side view of basic stance

Basic stance

USE OF SKI LIFTS

The use of Ski Lifts — T-bar drag tows, Poma lifts, etc.
— is part of learning to ski. Both pupil and Instructor
should bear the following important points in mind.

Getting on

Step round into the track with the minimum of delay.

Ensure skis are parallel and pointing up the line of the
lift.

Stand with feet apart — ready to slide forward in the
basic stance.

Hold both sticks in the outside hand, ready to take the
bar with the inside hand.

Take the bar and place on the seat, look forward and
be ready to take the initial pull with the hand and arm.

Do not sit on the bar or disc, take the pull gradually on
the seat flexing the legs and guiding the skis as when
skiing.

Getting off

At the getting off point step off to the side quickly,
clearing the area for the next skiers to arrive.

On T-bar Tows it is sometimes necessary for the skier
on the inside of the lift line to hold on to the bar until it
retracts into the housing as it rounds the wheel at the
top.

Read and follow the instructions of all lift signs.

SNOWPLOUGH GLIDE & BRAKE

The 'Snowplough' — with the skis spread apart in a 'V' angle uses the Basic Stance as an elementary means of controlling the gliding speed downhill. The novice skier begins to learn the use of the edges to slow down or direct the skis.

Snowplough

Basic Position
In the fall-line, with the legs displace the heels of both skis at an equal angle apart. The skis are spread open with the tips near together. The skier stands in the basic skiing stance — body held centrally and squarely between the skis, knees and ankles lightly flexed along the inside edges of the skis. Both skis are equally weighted.

Gliding Plough
In the glide the skis are flattened to the snow in a narrow plough angle. An upright stance is held over the gliding skis.

Braking Plough
By sinking down — pushing out the legs and feet — the ski heels are displaced into a wider plough angle. Pressure on the edges to spread out the ski heels effects braking on the snow.

Important Pointers

Spreading both skis out at an equal angle. Feeling edge control — as the skis are widened in the plough, the feet should feel braking on the inside edges.

Snowplough — Gliding and Braking

Narrow
Angle —
Gliding
Plough

Gliding —
High Stance

Braking —
Lowered Stance

Wider
Angle —
Braking
Plough

F L

25

Teaching Method — Snowplough Gliding & Braking

The Snowplough is the first basic controlling manoeuvre for the student, and once the stance has been acquired, should be progressed quickly into turning across the slope.

Teach first as a stationary exercise to feel the position.

Emphasise open legs spread, with body upright and the use of standing up and sinking down movements from the legs.

It is essential that the student feels gliding on the inside edges.

It is important that the student concentrates on allowing the skis to slide — using the Gliding Plough narrower angle of the skis. Over emphasis on the braking plough can put the pupil into a defensive attitude, skiing too slowly to progress on to the next stages.

Revise straight running into the plough glide.

Class Activity — when space allows, more than one pupil should practice at a time.

Terrain Easy gradient slope on prepared snow conditions.

Aids Short Skis.

Exercises

Stationary
1. Hopping or brushing out the ski heels into the snowplough angle.
2. Holding the Plough stance and rolling knees and ankles in and outwards to give edge feel.

Gliding
3. Straight Run start pushing out into a Gliding Plough.
4. Snowplough Glide by upstand, down to widen ski angle into Braking Plough.
5. Rythmic Gliding Plough to Braking Plough in succession.
6. Hopping out into Plough and back into Parallel in succession.
7. Rythmic opening and closing of legs to plough and run parallel.
8. Repeat exercises using slalom poles or ski stick as corridor markers.

Exercises — Snowplough Glide & Brake

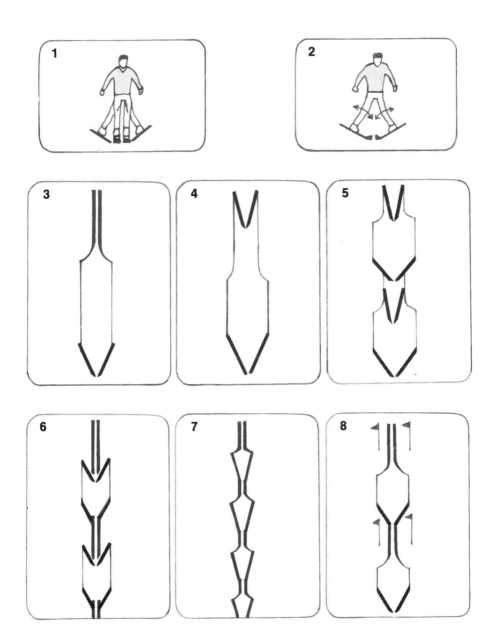

Common Faults

Inability to hold the Snowplough angle of the skis.

The causes can be through over-edging on the inside of the skis, opening only one leg out into the plough angle, and by pressing the knees in towards one another.

With ankle and knee flexed along the ski, the whole leg is spread sideways to push the heels open. Only sufficient pressure is applied on the inside edge to allow the skis to slideslip forwards, without catching an outside edge.

If necessary, the Instructor should hold the pupil's tips and ski backwards slowly to enable the learner to feel the correct position. Ski behind pupil, holding onto sticks helps them to form a plough without direct aid from Instructor.

Rigid Body Position

Arms are held tightly with the legs stiff and a tendency to sit too far back, pushing out only one leg.

Skis cross through over-edging.

Correct by maintaining a relaxed body stance with leg flexing, and exercise variety.

Too wide a Snowplough Angle — hips become locked, legs straighten and weight can go too far back. Skis are over-edged.

SNOWPLOUGH TURNS

By holding the Snowplough Position elementary slow-speed turns can be performed. Using leg turning action on either ski, the novice skier can steer down easy ski-runs. At the same time it teaches a feeling of using the legs and edges to control the skis.

Snowplough Turn

In the straight Snowplough Glide, a down motion is made by pressing the knee forward along the inside edge of the turning ski. Steering the ski by turning the leg and foot, together with setting of the inside edge. More weight pressure is applied to this ski by the leg action.

The upper body remains square to the direction of travel, with slight outward angulation when bending the leg more on the turning ski.

Linked Snowplough Turns are made by standing up in the Gliding position from the previous turn, skis equally weighted to turn into the fall-line. The turn can be assisted by a slight outward facing of the upper body. Turn in the opposite direction by pressing the knee along the inside edge of the outer ski, turning the foot and changing the weight pressure to this ski. Link by resuming a Gliding Plough position with equally weighted skis to turn into the fall-line.

Important Pointers —

In the Snowplough position both edges are set ready to be used for turning by either leg action. A relaxed flexing forward of the knees is made to apply foot turning pressure to the outside steering ski. Up and downsink movements to link the turns together, help in continuous turning down the fall-line.

Snowplough Turn

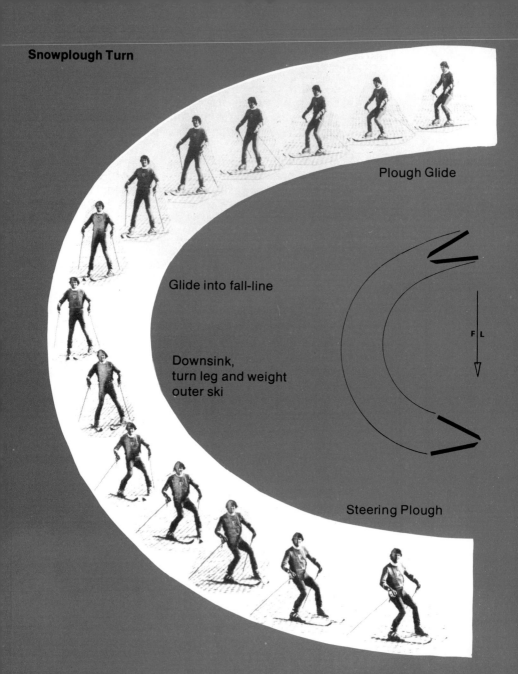

Plough Glide

Glide into fall-line

Downsink,
turn leg and weight
outer ski

F L

Steering Plough

Teaching Method — Snowplough Turns

The Snowplough should be progressed as soon as possible into a useful turning manoeuvre. Changing from standing on equally weighted skis to using the leg/foot turning action from ski to ski.

This elementary turn is the first major step in the pupils' progress, enabling them to become mobile down easy runs, and to use ski-lifts for practice.

Demonstrate that both ski edges are set ready to use for turning in either direction. Steering one ski with knee press and foot turning, as against the use of both knees to steer two edges later in parallel turns. A rotary action through the foot, steers the ski on its inside edge.

Emphasise leg and foot turning action, knee steering along the inside edge line of the ski, together with transfer of more weight pressure on the turning ski.

Up and down motions with leg turning/weight transfer to give rhythmic turning on alternate skis.

The use of the Gliding Plough stance with a narrow ski angle, rather than a wide braking plough, is again important.

Revise the Snowplough Glide and Braking as necessary.

Terrain

Easy gradient slope on prepared snow conditions.

Aids

Short Skis enable the skier to move easily, and give better control.

Exercises

1. Static leg/foot turning, with weight transfer, from one ski to the other with up and down movements.
2. Snowplough Glide with small heel pushes on alternate skis.
3. Gliding Plough with rhythmic pushing on one ski only to turn across the slope. Repeat on opposite ski.
4. Gliding Plough with one push out on turning ski. Repeat on opposite ski.
5. Repeat this exercise as a linked garland across the slope, standing up in the Gliding Plough to steer to the fall-line.
6. Linked Snowplough Turns emphasising turning of leg/foot, weight transfer and Gliding stance.
7. Snowplough Turns round Slalom Poles.
8. Shorter linked Snowplough Turns close to the fall-line.

Exercises — Snowplough Turns

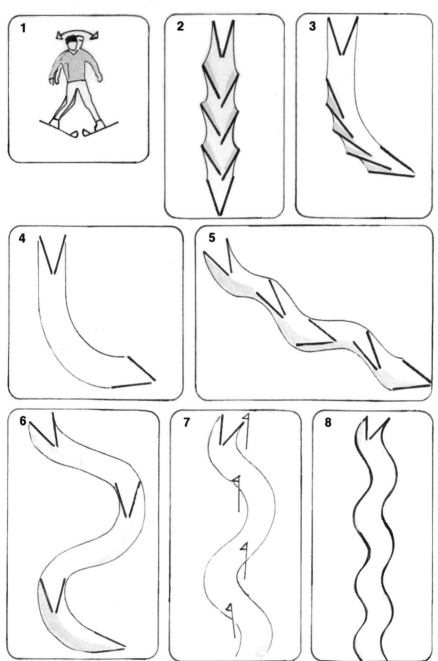

Common Faults   Loss of the Snowplough ski angle as the skis speed-up in the turn — the skier sits back as the skis turn downhill, allowing the skis to return parallel. A positive flexing of the ankle and knee over the turning ski must be held throughout the manoeuvre. The inside ski has less weight pressure, and is easier to hold in the open sliding position.

Flattening of the turning ski to skid out of the turn. Caused by not steering on the inside edge, straightening the leg to roll the boot outwards.

Moving the hips outwards and twisting the body in towards the turn — the inner leg and ski become weighted, losing the steering by the outer ski.

Correction Aids   Using ski sticks held out horizontally in front of the body, with straight arms.

Reaching down to touch outside boot heel, or reaching out to side.

Hand pressed behind turning knee.

Slalom Poles set at the outward angle of lean as an objective aid to avoid leaning into the centre of the turn.

Traversing — Basic Skiing Stance

Crossing the slope at any angle from the steepest line (fall-line) is 'Traversing' — and is the important basic skiing stance from which most ski manoeuvres are started.

Traversing uses the Basic Stance, setting the skis on edge to hold a tracking line across the snow. This edge set requires the lower ski to have more weight pressure applied by outward angulation of the upper body, with the uphill hip and leg pushed forward. For comfort and balance, the open stance position is used. Although the usual technical reference for Traversing is to cross the slope with parallel placed skis, it is possible for example, to ski a traverse line by Snowploughing.

Traversing

Skiing across the slope, skis tracking parallel. In the Basic Stance the skis are comfortably apart. Uphill ski advanced according to the amount the uphill leg and hip is pushed forward. The ankles and knees are flexed forwards and inwards to set the edges depending on the steepness of the slope. The upper body faces the direction of travel, with a slight outward angulation according to the slope angle. More weight is applied to the lower ski as the slope angle increases — on flatter ground and in deep snow both skis tend to be equally weighted. Arm, hand and stick position are held as in the Basic Skiing Stance.

Traversing across the slope

Basic traverse stance

Holding sticks outstretched
to give correct angulated
stance

Teaching Method — Traversing

Traversing is taught using the Basic Stance to ski across the slope and as a preparation for Parallel skiing. Skiing downhill requires speed control, and Traversing is one of the most important means of controlling speed. Modification of the Basic Skiing Stance is necessary to accommodate the tilted uphill hip and leg — everything on the uphill side being slightly advanced (shoulder, hip, leg, boot and ski). For stability it is easier to have slightly more weight on the lower ski angulating outward from the hips as the slope angle steepens pushing knees forward and into the slope enables a good edge set to be made for tracking the skis into the snow. Head held looking forwards.

Demonstrate and practice the position from a stand-still or sidestep uphill, emphasising the importance of edge setting, lower ski weighting and holding a natural stance.

Teach on a slope that will slow the skier down (rise or ridge), and stop by stepping uphill. Stopping can also be effected by Ploughing the lower ski, or skidding both ski heels downhill.

Revise side-stepping and straight running exercises where possible.

Terrain

Moderate gradient slope with natural runout if possible.

Aids

Open stance skis.

Exercises & Correction Aids

1. Knee pressing and flexing to set edges in shallow traverse line.
2. Reaching out with downhill stick to draw a line in the snow, palm of hand up.
3. Bending out to the side touch heel of downhill boot.
4. Lifting uphill ski heel off snow, replace and lift in succession.
5. Shallow traverse line, stepping skis uphill in parallel steps.
6. Hopping both ski heels off the snow, tips held in snow contact.
7. Stepping out uphill to stop from a steeper traverse line.

Exercises — Traversing

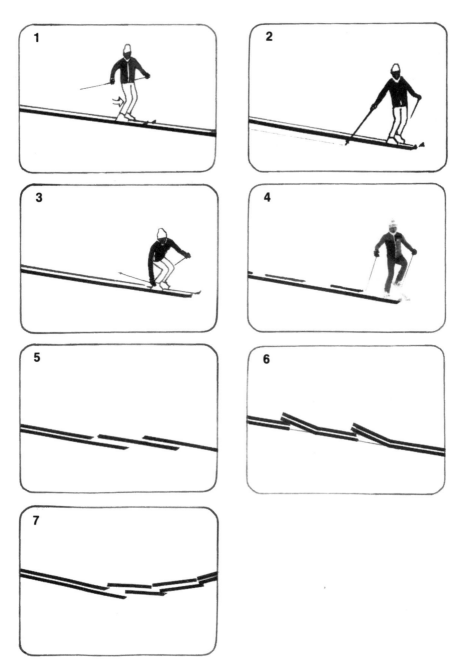

8. Using ski sticks held out in front of body to the slope angle, giving a reference objective line to hold the correct stance. Sticks fastened over hips, and sticks held behind head across the shoulders.

Common Faults

Skis Side-slip
Caused through insufficient edge bite. Requires more inward lean of lower leg, and feel of pressure on the correct part of the foot.

Leaning in towards the slope.
The upper body turned in towards the hiilside, with the hips turned outwards. The result is that the upper ski takes more weight, is pulled back, and tracking control on the lower ski is lost. Pupil must feel the correct Basic Stance before moving off across the slope.

SIDE-SLIPPING

When the skier is traversing, and allows the ski edges to release their tracking grip on the snow, they will skid sideways — or side-slip — down the slope.

As an exercise for feeling edge control, the side-slip can be practiced straight down the fall-line. But it is more useful and important for learning parallel skiing, by practicing the side-slip from moving across the slope. In this way, it is not only a useful exercise for skidding the skis parallel, but enables the skier to lose height or slow down without having to make a turn, such as on a steep pitch of a ski run.

Side-slip in the Fall-line

From a traverse position skis horizontal to the slope, a downsink motion is made with an outward facing of the upper body. The knees are pressed to the outside line of the skis, releasing the edge grip on the snow.

Control of the side-slip is by leg/foot action only, the upper body remains relaxed facing in the direction of travel.

Reset the edges by pressing the knees back inwards to the slope and stand up again.

Forward Diagonal Side-slip

From a traverse across the slope, the side-slip is initiated by downsink motion of the knees and ankles to release the ski edges. Control the side-slip by knee action, maintaining the lowered body position. The upper body faces in the direction the skis are slipping. The edges are reset by pressing the knees inwards to resume the traverse position.

The alternative method of initiating the side-slip is to make an up-stand preparation in the traverse, followed immediately by the downsink motion to release the ski edges with the knees and ankles.

Important Pointers

Stability in the side-slip by lowering the C of G by downsink movement. Important to hold the body angulation, weighting both skis, and maintaining upper ski lead. Reach with the hands in the direction of the side-slip.

Forward Side Slip

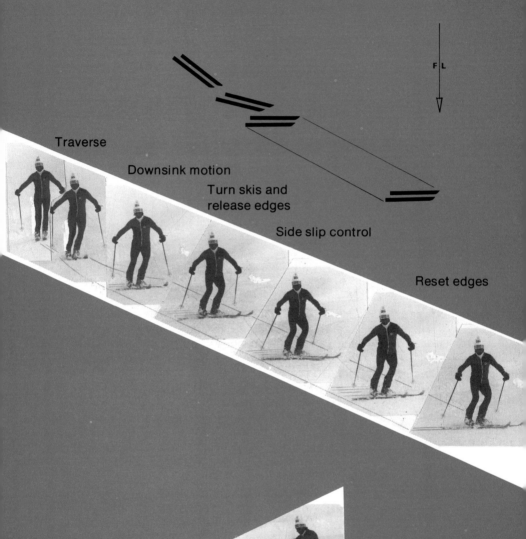

F | L

Traverse

Downsink motion

Turn skis and
release edges

Side slip control

Reset edges

Exercise using sticks outstretched
to maintain upper body
outward angulation in
direction of side slip

40

Teaching Method — Side-Slipping.

Side-slipping exercises are an introduction to parallel skiing. For practical skiing it is used for slowing down or stopping — having both ski edges to use, rather than just one ski as when Snowploughing.

For good demonstration, and class practice, it is particularly important to choose the right snow terrain.

A good Basic Traverse Position should be encouraged. Emphasising that the side-slip is a manoeuvre which uses only subtle play of the lower legs and feet to release the edges. Pressing the knees forward along the skis controls the setting of the edges on the snow. Rolling the knees out from the slope releases the edges — rolling the knees inwards re-sets the edges.

Side-slipping requires precise edge feel through the feet. Do not expect the students to perform side-slipping perfectly. The learner skier tends to use the whole body, hips in particular, to induce the release of the skis sideways.

The teaching progression uses static exercises, fall-line exercises skidding directly down the slope, and then into traverse forward side-slips across the slope.

Revise traversing.

Terrain

Smooth prepared snow conditions on at least a medium gradient slope.

Aids

Open stance ski position.

Exercises

Static between stick support
1. Slide top ski, then lower ski.
   Shuffle skid sideways both skis.
   Step up and skid both skis together sideways.

Fall-line
2. Pushing with ski sticks on uphill side.
3. Skid lower ski then upper ski down fall-line.
   Shuffling both skis.
4. Both skis skidded by lower leg/knee in and out action.
5. Hopping both skis downhill into skid.
6. Forward and backward skidding in zig-zag through poles.

Forward from traverse

7. Sliding lower ski into the diagonal skid.
   Shuffling both skis into forward side-slip.
8. Traverse and emphasise upstand into downsink and sideslip.
   Small hops to skid skis into forward sideslip.
9. Linked forward side-slips in succession across the slope.
10. From a steeper traverse line, turning the feet with downsink into diagonal sideslip.
11. Sideslipping through corridor or single markers of slalom poles.

Common Faults

Hips are moved outwards away from the slope. Causing weight pressure to be shifted to the upper ski, the ski heels break away losing control of the side-slip.

Catching of lower ski outside edge. The skis are flattened too much by insufficient ankle and knee bend forward along the ski.

Ensure that the pupil maintains knee and ankle bend from the downsink to give just enough release to allow the skis to side-slip.

Correction Aids

Stand below student and pull sideways downhill from extended ski sticks. Student should resist the pull in order to feel the effect of edging and release by pressing knees in and out sideways.

Holding sticks out horizontally in the direction of the side-slip to prevent hips from twisting outwards.

Exercises — Sideslipping

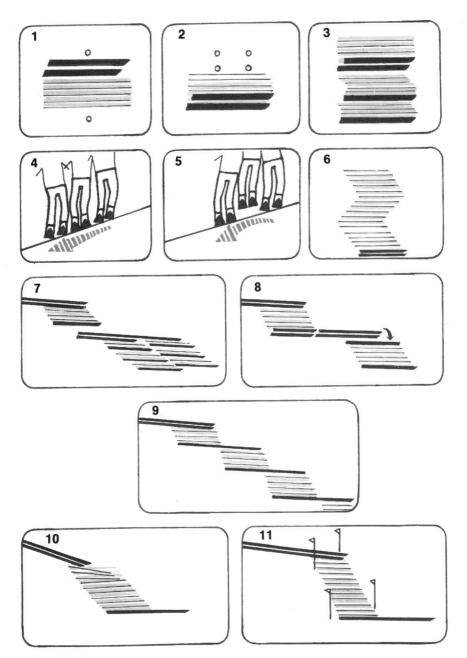

SWING TO THE HILL

The Swing to the Hill — or Uphill Swing — is a parallel turn across the slope. It is an important exercise in the progression to full Parallel Turns.

The skier will find that this is the main stopping manoeuvre, either quickly from the traverse or from the completion of a turn.

The steering effect learned in the Snowplough Turn is now made with both legs and feet to steer the skis uphill.

Swing to the Hill

From the traverse, with down motion, release the edges to initiate a narrow curving side-slip swing across the slope.

The length of the swing is controlled by edge setting and knee steering. Turning action is from lower legs and feet. Angulation of the upper body maintains pressure on the ski edges.

To resume a traverse line, straighten up to reset the edges.

As an aid to initiating the swing, an up motion can be made prior to the downsink steering movement, particularly when the Uphill Swing is being performed directly down the fall-line.

Important Pointer

Feel the steering effect by pushing the knees forward and to the inside of the swing. The legs and feet are twisted in the direction the skis are to be turned.

Outward angulation of the upper body keeps the weight over the lower ski.

Swing to the Hill

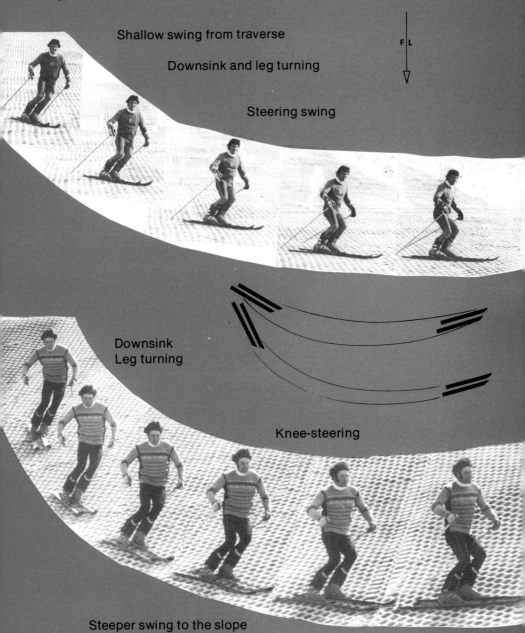

Shallow swing from traverse

Downsink and leg turning

Steering swing

F L

Downsink
Leg turning

Knee-steering

Steeper swing to the slope

Teaching Method — Swing to the Hill.

As a teaching progression, the Uphill Swing is introduced to the pupil from not too steep a traversing line. This elementary swing is a steered curving side-slip, and exercises lead directly to the end phase of the Basic Swing turn. Open stance ski position helps to feel the skidding and steering with both ski edges.

Emphasise turning legs and feet, together with knee steering of the swing.

Demonstrate angulation exercises.

Encourage the pupil to allow the skis to run and not over-turn the skis too quickly.

In Section 4, the Fan Method uses the Uphill Swing to progress into Parallel Turns.

Revise traversing and side-slipping.

Terrain
Preferably a moderate gradient slope with large convex shaped hump. Ideally the terrain will help the skier to turn uphill.

Aids
Correctly chosen terrain. Objective turning around a Slalom Pole.

Exercises
1. Traverse and into side-slip by turning feet and skis into the skid.
2. Traverse steeper line turning skis into side-slip then steering out of side-slip.
3. Traverse into uphill swing.
4. Successive uphill swings, turning the skis downhill from each swing by stepping out and together or by a narrow plough.
5. Hopping the ski heels downhill into the uphill swing.
6. Hop from plough into parallel swing.
7. Longer parallel uphill swings.

Common Faults
Swinging the shoulders round to face into the slope.
Caused by rotating the upper body, moving the hips outwards.
The upper body must remain facing outwards relative to the direction of the swing.

Overturning the skis.
Caused by allowing the ski heels to slide downhill, without pushing the knees forward.

Correction aids
Reaching out with hand and stick to the outside of the swing — giving outward angulation of the body.
Holding sticks horizontal out front, stopping rotation.

Exercises — Swing to the Hill

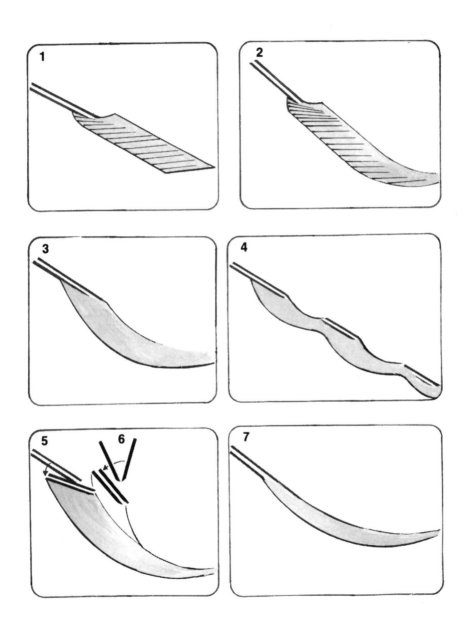

BASIC SWING

The Basic Swing is an intermediate turning manoeuvre, using the Snowplough Glide at the start and
complete the turn with the skis in a Parallel Swing.

As a practical turn it gives the novice skier the feeling
of skidding out of the fall-line with the skis parallel. It is
less tiring to perform than continuously Snowploughing, allowing the skier to let the skis run faster. At the
same time in the open stance using both feet for
stability and edge control.

Basic Swing

From the Basic Stance in the traverse, open both skis
out into a Snowplough Glide with up motion. The skis
are equally weighted and turned into the fall-line,
assisted if necessary, by an outward facing of the hips
and upper body. In the fall-line, transfer weight pressure to the outside ski, close the inner ski parallel to
the outer ski, combined with a down sink motion of the
legs. Turning the legs and feet, steering by pressing
the knees forward into the swing, and angulating the
body outwards to weight the outer ski — the turn is
completed from the fall-line with a parallel swing.

Important Pointers

Closing the skis into the open parallel skid with a down
sinking movement of the legs. Close the inner ski into
a slightly forward position — as in any traverse or
swing stance.

To feel a smooth slide-in of this inner ski, push the
inside knee forwards which will help in the flattening
and rolling on to the outside edge of this closing ski.

The skis can be hopped parallel from the plough, if it is
difficult to slide in the inner ski.

The Basic Swing

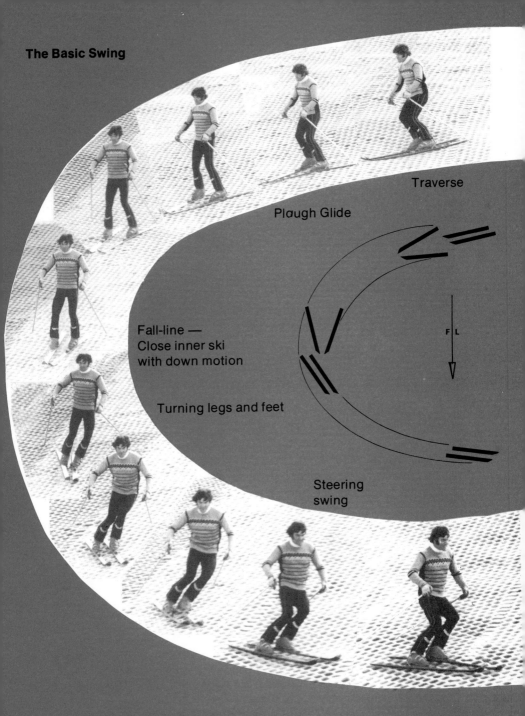

Traverse

Plough Glide

Fall-line —
Close inner ski
with down motion

Turning legs and feet

Steering
swing

F L

49

Teaching Method — Basic Swings

Teaching Basic Swings is the transitional stage into Parallel Turns. For the learner it is a very practical turn, which gives them still 'two footed' steering control throughout the swing, with both edges working for them in the parallel swing out of the fall-line. In this way, with the skis in the basic stance — open but parallel — the student can allow the skis to travel faster, but still remain in balanced control.

The important phase in the turn, is combining the down motion with the closing of the skis leading to the parallel swing across the slope. Steering the outside ski with down motion and skidding-in the inner ski smoothly by turning the leg and foot — feeling inner to outer edge change.

The turn can be broken down into the phases:—
Basic Traverse — Plough Glide — Parallel Swing

Teach exercises for feeling the closing of the inner ski parallel from the Gliding Plough stance. Lead into longer swing exercises, using the Plough Glide as a start — Plough Swings — until the pupil Ploughs down the fall-line into the swing. Garland linked Plough Swings are important to give rhythmic practice of upstand in the Plough to downsink closing skis in the parallel swing.

Progress into the actual turn, encouraging continuous linked turning movements down the fall-line without traversing between turns.

The student should now have sufficient competence to ski faster and negotiate standard and intermediate ski-runs.

Revise traversing/side-slip and swing to the hill exercises, from Gliding Plough.

Terrain

Moderate gradient slope on packed snow — a convex hump is useful for closing the skis into the parallel swing.

Aids

Short skis.

Exercises

1. Static — support on sticks from a plough stance down the slope — close inner ski to lower ski.
2. Plough traverse, closing upper ski to lower ski.
3. Plough traverse, closing upper ski to lower with downsink into a short side-slip swing.

50

Exercises — Basic Swing

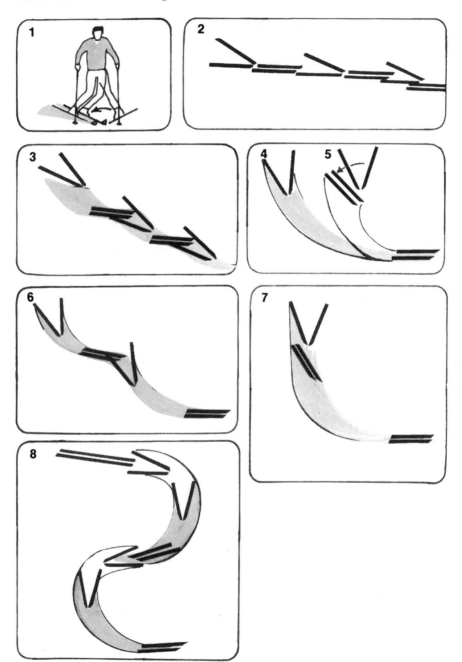

4. Plough turn steeper down slope, close upper ski into swing back across the slope. Up, down motions.
5. As No. 4 but using a hop to close upper ski into swing.
6. Successive Plough Swings, in garland form to both sides, progressively into the fall-line.
7. Basic Swing from fall-line in both directions.
8. Linked Basic Swings with no traverse between turns.

Common Faults

Unable to close inner ski into parallel swing. Pupil fails to transfer turning weight pressure to outside ski. Also rotation of shoulders (hips) holds weight on inner ski.

Too wide a plough angle. Also makes it more difficult to skid in inner ski smoothly until well through the fall-line. Narrow Plough Glide angle essential for speed and smooth closing of skis.

Insufficient up and down motion by leg extension and bending leads to a rigid stance over the skis, stepping in too quickly of inner ski, and turning by body rotation power. Use exercises that give the pupil timing of the correct flexing movements to initiate and control the turn.

Correction Aids

Holding sticks out horizontally in front of the body to ensure turning movements and skidding is effected by lower leg only.
Reaching out to the outside in the parallel swing.
Ski stick frame across the hips — indicating any excessive hip rotation.
Slalom Pole turning down the fall-line.

BASIC PARALLEL TURNS — TEACHING METHODS

Basic Swing — Basic Parallel Turns (Standard Method)

Snowplough Turns — Narrow Plough — Basic Parallel Turns (Direct Method)

Swing to the Hill progression — Basic Parallel Turns (Fan Method)

PARALLEL TURNS

The aim of the basic learning progression, is to have the novice skier perform turns where the skis remain parallel throughout the turn. Skiing parallel in this way gives the skier the use of both legs and feet for changing the edges, and turning the skis at the same time.

It is the stage from which the skier can use the skills acquired to become an accomplished performer — ready to perfect parallel skiing and ski most downhill terrain safely.

Basic Parallel Turn

The Basic Parallel Turn uses the open stance ski position for stability throughout the turn. From the traverse a prepared setting of the edges is made. The turn is initiated by upmotion, flexing the legs to unweight the skis. At the same time both skis are flattened and turned by the legs and feet. Both edges are changed with a downsink motion of the legs, pushing the knees forward to steer the swing. The inner ski is advanced as the skis are turned. The upper body is angulated outwards to maintain steering or carving of the edges by the legs and feet. As the turn is completed, stand up to resume a new traverse line.

Important Pointers

The Parallel Turn is 'triggered off' instantly with both feet — if a step or stem occurs then the turn is not technically 'parallel'. Both skis must flatten and change edges together. The preparation into the start of the turn is important so that both legs can work as a single unit to turn the skis.

Steering of the skis through the turn arc is made by pressing the knees forward along the inside edges.

Basic Parallel Turn

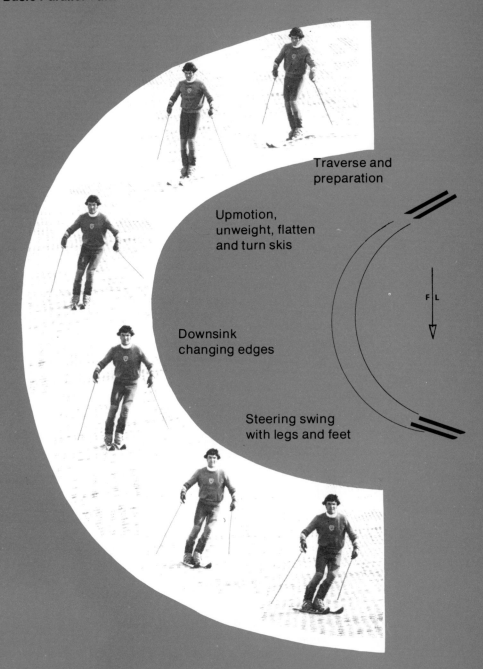

Traverse and preparation

Upmotion, unweight, flatten and turn skis

Downsink changing edges

Steering swing with legs and feet

F L

Teaching Method — Basic Parallel Turn, standard method from Basic Swing

The student is progressed into Basic Parallel Turns by refining the Basic Swing. Emphasis should be to narrow the Gliding Plough angle of the skis, with the use of a more pronounced down-up-down sink motion to initiate the turn. The up-motion should be a definite movement, demonstrated to unweight the skis by an upward extension of the body.

Class exercising can use successive garland narrow plough swings, where the plough is gradually lessened and more down-up-down movements are used with legs and feet action to turn in and out of the fall-line.

Garland exercises can be used until the skier is performing open stance parallels, turning both skis downhill on the upmotion followed by downsink of the legs to steer the swing back across the slope. These exercises in garland form give rhythm of movement and repetitive feel to the importance of 'flowing' the actions necessary to initiate parallel turns.

Teach by linking turns in practice, narrowing the plough and closing the skis together before the fall-line, until eventually open stance parallels are being made in rough form. Using lifts for continual running is essential as the feeling of turning is always easier after several turns have been made in rhythm. If the student cannot eliminate the stem, then hopping ski heel exercises can be introduced as in the Fan Method. Once the skier has a fair grasp of the essential basic parallel turning movements, then introduce the stick plant as a turning aid.

Revise — side-slipping in the basic stance, uphill swings, basic swings.

Terrain

Moderate steep slopes. Use of small bumps to help turning.

Aids

Short skis. Small bumps to initiate turns. Slalom poles.

Exercises

1. Basic Swing Turns, narrowing the plough angle down and closing the skis together progressively earlier than the fall-line.
2. Narrow Gliding Plough Swings into open Parallel Swing garlands.
3. Open stance Parallel Turns of varied radius.
4. Hopping ski heels exercises to initiate turns.
5. Introduce use of ski stick plant as an aid to turning.

Exercises — Basic Parallel Turns

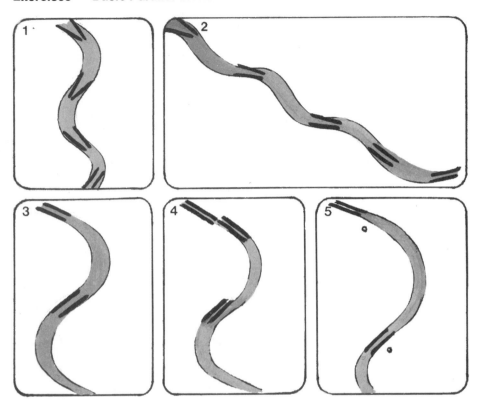

Common Faults	**Incorrect preparation before the turn is started.** Results in stemming, or loss of smooth initiation of the turn with both feet. **Unco-ordinated movements to induce the turn.** The correct sequence of movements are necessary, performed smoothly and uninterrupted, in order to flatten then re-edge the skis. Only one ski edge changed results in a stem or catching inside edge. **Poor Swing Control** Starting the turn correctly, but not enough down sink and leg turning action steer the skis correctly through the fall-line and across the slope. May result in rotation of hips and lower ski breaking away.
Correction Aids	Slalom Pole Markers. Use the hop to unweight, flatten and turn the skis. Reaching out to angulate to the side in the swing.

Section 3 — Direct Method into Parallel Turns.

This alternative method into the Parallel skiing, is introduced as a result of developments in the teaching system.

Over the past few years, design changes in equipment has had a significant effect on the novice skier's learning progress. Short Skis are easier to turn and skid, together with modern boots that give a positive edge response to the actions of the skier's feet and legs.

Also influencing the use of the Direct Method, is the fact that some learners acquire the fundamental skills quicker, enabling them to turn the skis in basic parallel swing after only a few hours' instruction. The requirement from the pupil is the ability to perform short Snowplough Turns linked together close to the fall-line, and at a reasonable speed. For example, younger skiers who are not afraid to let the skis move downhill and have good reflex action.

The exercise progression is straightforward, emphasising using rhythmic turning of the legs and feet in short turns down the fall-line. It is suited, therefore, to Scottish-type gully skiing where the runs are narrow, and necessary to turn continuously near to the fall-line.

In the practical teaching situation, the class is instructed more on continually moving downhill, rather than exercising just one or two linked turns. However, in the Teaching Assessment Exam the student Instructor would be expected to demonstrate and teach the correct flow of exercises on a more confined area of snow.

Revise :— Smooth Snowplough Turns; Basic Skiing Stance, Leg/Feet Turning.

Terrain

Easy gradient slopes on packed snow conditions. Small bumps in the fall-line.

Aids

Short Skis. Use of a Trainer Ski Tow. Slalom Poles for objective Turning.

DIRECT METHODS —

Gliding Plough
Short turns in fall-line

Narrowing Plough in
Rhythmic turning pattern

Gradual closing skis
into Basic Parallel
short turns

F L

Exercises	1. Linked Snowplough Turns of short radius close to the fall-line — with a positive weight transfer from outer ski to outer ski, and leg/foot action on turning ski.

1. Linked Snowplough Turns of short radius close to the fall-line — with a positive weight transfer from outer ski to outer ski, and leg/foot action on turning ski.
2. Linked narrow Gliding Plough short turns to the fall-line — with weight transfer and more up and down motion from leg flexing.
3. Snowplough Wedel Turns in the fall-line — with a quicker transfer weight pressure to outer ski in rapid succession. More up and down motion leg flex.
4. Linked Gliding Plough short turns into short Basic Swings — with weight transfer, more up and down motion leg flex and partial skidding with both feet.
5. Linked short Basic Swings into open Parallel Turns — pronounced up and down motion with leg flex into turning both feet in an open stance.
6. Linked short Basic Parallel Turns close to fall-line — holding the same turning rhythmic pattern, turning of both skis in open stance with emphasised up and down motion from leg flex.
7. Static Exercise from stick support in fall-line — plough stance closing inner ski as outer ski is stepped across — with rhythmic transfer stepping and leg turning action.
8. Introducing the use of stick plant to the same pattern of linked turning excercises — with correctly co-ordinated up and down motions to use the stick as an aid to turning.

Common Faults

Losing the rhythm of close linked turns. Results in the skier making longer radius swings, and holding the Plough too long.

Too static over the skis, making it difficult to convert the Plough into flowing skidding of both skis by not enough up-down flexing movement.

Braking on the edges. Loses rhythm, causes over-turning and slows the skier down. A good flowing tempo of leg/feet turning essential.

Correction Aids

Slalom Poles vertically down the fall-line.
Ski Sticks held horizontally in front of body down the slope.

Exercises — Direct Method Parallel Turns

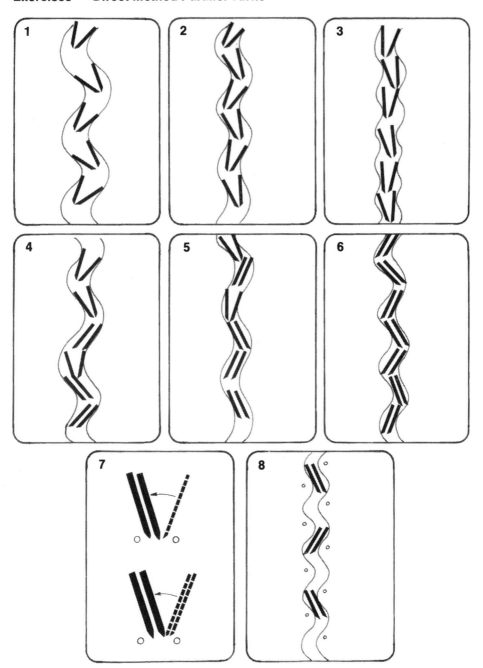

Section 4 — Fan Method of teaching Parallel Turns.

This teaching method into the Basic Parallel Turn, uses the Swing to the Hill as a main exercise progression, turning the skis by successive Uphill Swings from across the slope, then into the fall-line, and finally as a turn through the fall-line.

As an alternative method, it is intended for use in practice where a student has difficulty in eliminating the stemmed out Plough ski stance — usually with one ski only. It can also be used as an adjunct to the standard method, requiring only a small area of snow on which to conduct the progression system of 'fan swings' — useful also for the Instructor when snow may be at a premium, and any patch of the correct terrain can be used to teach the Parallel Turn.

As the name suggests, the exercise progression produces a pattern of tracks in the form of a 'Fan' made to either side by increasing the angle of traverse into the uphill swing.

Emphasise a high stand into the down sink motion to induce the skidding and turning of the skis round the swing, especially in the fall-line. The crux of the fan method is the first shallow turn from the opposite traverse line — emphasise downsink prior to upstand to flatten the skis into the previous pattern of uphill swings. To ensure that the student keeps a 'parallel feel' to turning of the skis, or to eliminate any stemming of the skis, hopping of the ski heels can be introduced. Teach hopping exercises across the slope — keeping the unweighting action produced by the heel hop to the minimum. Used in the turn proper as a means of initiating the turn, the hop should be reduced to the standard down-up-down leg turning flex without heel lift as soon as the student has a grasp of the basic parallel turn.

The class can be kept active by practicing swings alternatively from opposite sides, perhaps using a slalom pole as a turning marker.

Revise — Traverse Basic Stance, Snowplough Turns, Side-slipping.

Terrain

Large convex hump preferably on a moderate gradient slope.

Aids

Short Skis, correct shaped terrain, Hopping heels of skis exercises.
Slalom Poles for objective turning.

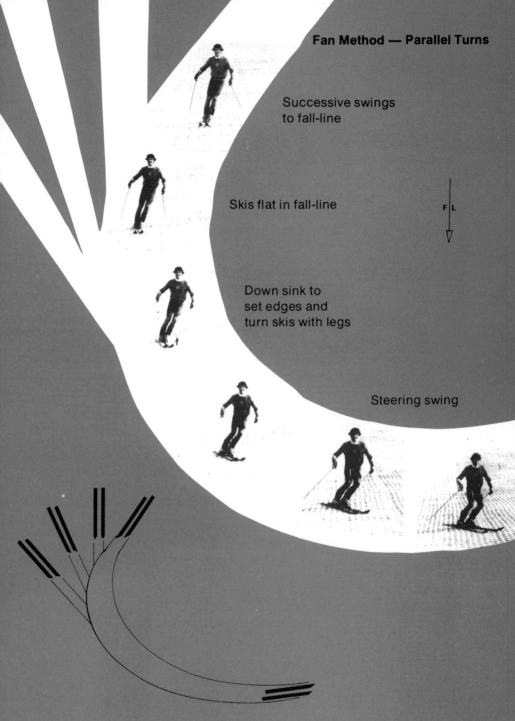

Fan Method — Parallel Turns

Successive swings
to fall-line

Skis flat in fall-line

F L

Down sink to
set edges and
turn skis with legs

Steering swing

Exercises	1. Uphill Swings from diagonally across the slope as an introduction (angle of lead in as used for Basic Swings).
	2. Steepening traverse until Fall-line, using pronounced upstand and downsink to steer the swing.
	3. Lead-in away from the fall-line as a shallow turn, important to stress downset, upmotion and downsink as skis flatten and change edges.
	4. Hopping exercises — First in traverse hopping heels only, then hopping uphill to skid back into traverse. The same exercise can be taught in the fall-line if the terrain is not too steep — heels first hopped straight, then from side to side.
	5. Increase the traverse angle into the Parallel Swing, using hopping of the heels if necessary to initiate the turn.
	6. Link parallel turns together.
	7. Introduce the use of the ski stick as an aid to turning.

Common Faults

Insufficient preparation to induce turning of both legs and feet at the same time.
Results in stemming of the skis, with a possible overturning by rotation of upper body off lower stemmed ski. Prior upstand necessary to use a good flex down and forwards to control the steering.

Trying to turn too quickly
Unco-ordinated movements. The Fan Method requires smooth flowing uphill swings, allowing the skis to do the work. Too hurried actions lead to an unbalanced position on the skis, and inability to make the required turning movements of legs and feet.
Locking knees together results in rotation of hips and stiffness of legs.

Correction Aids

Reaching out with stick and arm to the side
Upper body facing down the slope — sticks held out in front.
Hopping exercises to fan the ski heels.
Multi-hop parallels — continual hops round the turn.

Exercises — Fan Method Parallel Turns

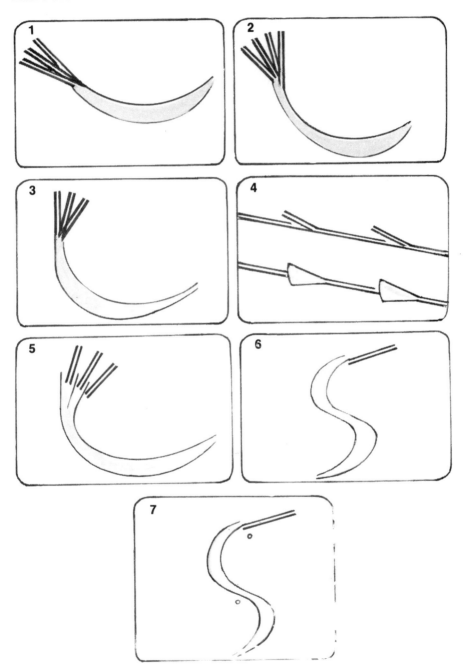

Section 5 — PARALLEL TURN WITH STICK PLANT.

The standard Parallel Turn is initiated by the same co-ordinated movements of edge set leg flex, followed immediately with an up-motion to flatten and turn the legs and skis, into a down sink to steer the skis in the turning arc.

The ski stick is planted on the downhill side of the skis (or the inside of the turn) at the moment of edge set or leg flex before the skis are turned. The stick is then immediately ready to use for the unweighting action by up-motion, as a direct support for the skier or as an aid to timing the unweighting and leg turning movements to initiate the turn.

With practice the skier will become more skilled in the use of co-ordinated leg and stick planting movements for turning the skis. The open stance Basic Parallel Turns will also become refined to ski more with the feet closer.

Parallel Turn with Stick Plant

From the Basic Stance in the Traverse, a prepared setting of the edges with leg down flex is made. At the same time the Ski Stick is planted on the downhill side comfortably at arm's reach — back from the tip and away from the side of the lower ski. The stick is planted positively to aid the successive up motion of the body to initiate the flattening and turning of the skis downhill by turning legs and feet. The turn is completed as before, changing the edges, and a down sink motion by pushing the knees forward to control the swing, angulating out the upper body as necessary over the lower ski to give edge steering.

Important Pointers

Use the correct length of ski stick to give a comfortable plant into the snow. Too long or too short will affect the timing.

It is also most important that the skier should understand clearly, that the stick plant is made always **before** the turn starts.

Parallel Turn with Stick Plant

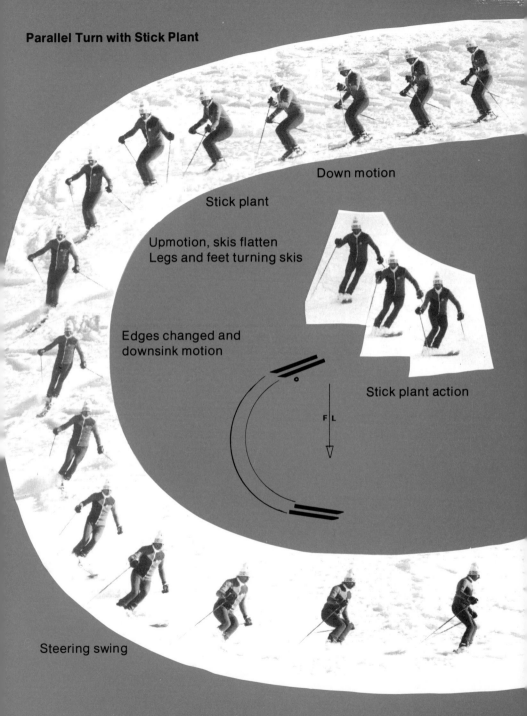

Down motion

Stick plant

Upmotion, skis flatten
Legs and feet turning skis

Edges changed and
downsink motion

Stick plant action

F L

Steering swing

Linked Parallel Turns

Downsink and
stick plant

Upmotion with
leg and feet
turning action

Knee
steering

Downsink
and stick
plant

Turning action

Steering to
link next
turn

Parallel Turns with little edge-set

Teaching Method — Introducing use of the Ski Stick Plant

In teaching the Stick Plant action it should be stressed that the Basic Stance is the key to efficient use of the planted stick. The hand and arm position in front of the body and just over shoulder width apart, gives the correct preparation to start the movement. Swing the stick forward by wrist action only, and the minimum of arm lift. With leg flex as the stick is swung forward, the stick point will touch and plant in the snow automatically.

The actual planted position on the snow should be in an area behind the ski-tip and away from the side of the ski — if the correct arm position is held, then the stick will be in the snow approximately 12" behind the tip and at least 6" away from the ski side. Planting the stick further away from the ski and back from the tip, gives a pretwist of the upper body — or anticipation — used to refine parallel skiing further.

The amount of pressure used to push on the stick from the moment of plant, depends on the degree of unweighting required to initiate the turn. Short sharp turns or bad snow conditions may require a strong grip and push off the stick to aid lifting the skis out of the snow. Long smooth turns may require only a mere touch of the stick, used more for timing the leg action.

Demonstrate the stick plant action statically, first with leg flex then with a good upspring to hop the ski heels.

Teach exercises in the traverse — leg flex with stick plant and hop, then with hop to displace ski heels uphill. On flatter terrain, the stick plant action can be taught down the fall-line, planting the pole rhythmically to right and left with hops, and then hopping the heels to the sides. Refine the parallel turn further to cut out the hop, and vary the turn radius.

All three methods of teaching parallel turns come together at this stage.

Introduce and teach in the basic parallel turn proper, according to which method the Instructor is using.

Revise — Basic Stance, Traversing, Uphill Swing, Parallel Turn.

Terrain

As for teaching Parallel Turns. Moderately easy slope for fall-line exercises.

Aids

Correct length of ski stick. Saying out loud the movements — "down" (plant) — "up".

Exercises

1. Static — Basic Stance with leg flex, stick plant into a push off and hop on the spot.
2. Traverse shallow line, flex and plant; flex, plant and hop; flex, plant, hop and displace ski heels uphill.
3. Introduce into the Basic Parallel Turn with hop.
4. Basic Parallel Turn without hop, but with upward motion keeping skis in contact with the snow on unweighting.
   or : —
5. Fall-line exercises on shallow slope. Basic Running Stance with leg flex and stick plant alternatively right and left. Progressing to hop heels off the planted stick, then to hop the ski heels to the opposite side of the planted stick. This sequence of alternative plant and hops to be made in rhythm and good down-up-down leg flex.
6. Progress stick plant into basic parallels linked together, or in fall-line skidding into short linked turns.

Common Faults

Not timing the stick plant to co-ordinate with leg flex. Results in the stick being planted too late, losing the full effect of triggering the turn.

Reaching too far forward to plant the stick. Overswinging the stick beyond the ski-tip, produces a loss of timing and shoulder rotation, making the turn clumsy to perform.

Holding onto the stick after the turn has started. The hand should stay forward of the body as the skier turns downhill, not allowing the hand and shoulder to be pulled back off the planted stick.

Correction Aids

Holding uphill stick across front of body in both hands, pivotting lower stick in stick plant, in traverse.

Repeated saying out loud the timing of stick plant — "down" — "up" or by numbers etc.

Exercises — Parallel Turn with Stick

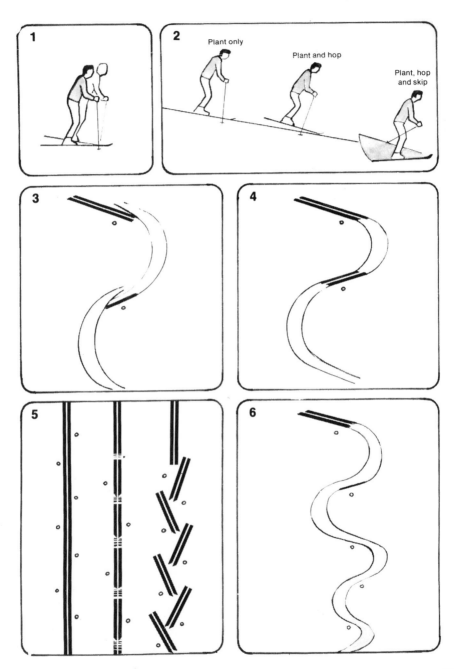

1

2 Plant only

Plant and hop

Plant, hop
and skip

3

4

5

6

Section 6 —

SHORT SWINGS

Skiing down steeper slopes it is necessary to control the descent by shortening the radius of the turn.

In this way the turn becomes tighter, so that the skier is quickly braking with both edges. In performing short swings, the normal turning actions are more pronounced and made in a quicker sequence. In extreme form these movements are a continuous edge change and rebound with both legs to turn from side to side. The essentials are continual flex-turning of the legs with exact timing of the stick plant, feeling the setting of the edges to hold the speed in check.

Edge-checks are also an excellent exercise to sharpen-up body control and reflex action, coupled with use of planted sticks.

Basic Short Swings

From a pronounced edge set check, a short parallel swing is made, together with the co-ordinated use of stick plant from an outward facing of the upper body. Support from the stick aids the rebound unweighting reaction to turn the skis with the legs and feet. The upper body maintains generally an outward facing position throughout the sequence of turns. After the rebound of the skis from the edge set, the outside ski is weighted with a strong forward pressure of the knees in the turning direction. At the same time, the outer arm and stick is brought downhill ready to plant with the next edge set with upper body anticipation. The skis are in the basic open stance, closing them together as the skier becomes more proficient.

The movements in Short Swings are in total motion — linking one edge set, plant and rebound into the next turn, directly down the fall-line.

On flatter slopes less emphasis of setting the edges is required. The stick plant becomes more of a timing aid as the skis roll over from edge to edge. The turns are smooth and near the fall-line, such rhythmic linked turns are called 'Wedeln'.

Important Pointers

Exact planting of the stick at the moment of edge set, so that the Skier can obtain the maximum support from the stick. The position where the stick is planted is also important — if the Skier is holding the correct outward facing body position then the arms will plant the stick in a line laterally downhill from the boots.

Short Swings require a vigorous work out-put of the legs to turn the skis continuously.

SHORT SWINGS —

F | L

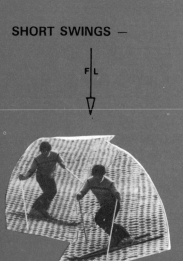

Edge to Edge checks with stick plant

Continuous linked downsink —
edge set — stick plant — rebound —
short swings

Teaching Method — Basic Short Swings

The student skier who has progressed to this learning stage, must have confidence to ski linked parallel turns on steeper slopes. A good sense of balance, feeling for the snow and skis should have been developed as a requirement to lead into Short Swings. The attitude of the skier has to be positive, with general physical fitness playing an important part in the approach to more advanced parallel skiing.

Exercises that use rhythmic leg play, edge setting and stick plant form the progression into the final linked swings down the fall-line. Traversing exercises similar to those given for introducing the stick plant are used, emphasising a more vigourous use of checking with the edges, together with equally stronger planting of the stick. The lower legs are cranked in towards the slope as a sharp pressing movement to get the maximum bite with the ski edges, creating a platform from which to flex and rebound the skis into the turn.

Turning Action — Edge Set — Stick Plant — Rebound

The co-ordinated use of the stick plant requires the hand and arm to be brought forward ready to jab the stick into the snow — a good wrist action and firm grip on the stick being essential.

Teaching is done in practice by continual running — choosing the best line of slope so that several swings are performed to get a good rhythm of holding the same speed and evenness of turns.

Revise — Close linked parallel turns. Use of the ski stick.

Terrain

Moderate to steep gradient slopes.

Aids

Short Skis. Correct length of ski sticks.

Exercises — Short Swings

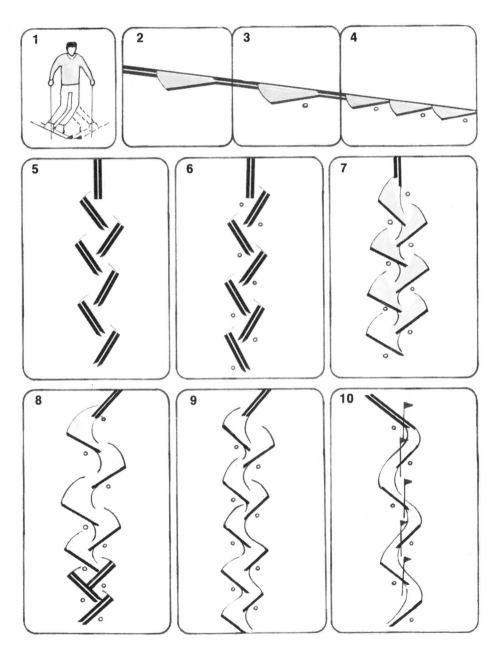

Exercises

1. Static — Hopping both ski heels from side to side, using stick support. Facing downhill on moderate slope or on flat.
2. Edge-set checks in the traverse. Small skids of heels downhill to edge-set and rebound into traverse. Without use of sticks.
3. As above exercise — continuous edge-set checks in traverse, but using downhill stick plant.
4. Faster tempo edge-set checks in traverse, as a continuous skid-check-rebound leg and feet turning action with correct stick use.
5. On shallow slope, hop checks from side to side, in fall-line.
6. As above exercise but introducing stick plant correctly co-ordinated with checks.
7. On steeper slope, down fall-line, pronounced edge-set checks and rebound, with correctly planted sticks.
8. Fall-line exercises varying swing skid into the check, from longer skids to checks side to side without skidding. Emphasising no loss of rhythm or delay in rebound from the edge-set.
9. Fall-line short swings reducing the amount of heel bounce or hop until short swings are made without heel lift, only by turning legs and feet.
18. Fall-line skiing through vertically set pattern of slalom poles.

Common Faults

Lack of positive edge-set check for rebound to turn the skis. Caused by lack of feel and turning action from the feet and legs.

Unsynchronised movements to maintain flow of short swings. By not planting the Stick in time, the skier is completely out of phase with the leg action to perform smoothly linked turns.

Not facing down the slope throughout the movements — allowing the hips to be thrown outwards in the turns.

Correction Aids

All "Edge-set-rebound" exercises with and without stick plant. Closed and wide track.

Slalom pole corridor or vertical patterns of poles to commit the pupil to edge control and hold the correct line.

Narrow plough in fall-line — quick edge setting from one ski to the other ski.

Section 7 — COMPRESSION TURNS

The development of parallel skiing over bumpy or 'mogulled' ski runs, using the bumps directly to aid turning, is the outcome of adapting technique to terrain. The Compression Turn is one such turn specifically used for skiing over undulated terrain. Compensation for the tracking of the skis over the bumps and hollows is made by bending and stretching the legs. It is the folding of the legs that the technique has its importance in turning around the humps and 'ironing out' the irregular shape of the terrain. In this way the legs absorb the bumps with the upper body having the minimum of up and down movement, giving rise to the term 'compression' action by the legs. The skis are not turned by unweighting action as in the parallel turn. Instead, the strong leverage action that is obtained through the legs and feet in the folded position, is used when the skis are on the crest of the bump. At this point the tips and heels of the skis have very little pressure on the snow — the skier's weight being applied only on the centre sections of the skis. Using a swivelling movement of the knees about the feet, it is then not difficult to pivot both skis around the top of the bump to change direction, using the ski stick as a direct support.

Once the skis are steered around the crest of the bump, and are sliding into the next hollow, then the legs are stretched out to follow the slope contour.

Turning in this manner requires a sharper perceptual response from the skier — looking forward to the terrain ahead and 'reading' the best line and turning points.

Compression Turn

Approaching the crest of a bump, or from a line across the slope, the legs are folded under the body. The ski stick is planted on the crest. Maintaining support from the stick, both skis are equally weighted, steering them downhill by twisting the legs and feet.

The skis pivot about the feet, while holding the folded or 'compressed' position with the legs and body. When the skis have been turned by the legs towards the fall-line the outer ski is weighted. The upper body bends forward from the planted stick and the legs are stretched out to resume the normal basic skiing stance. The amount of leg extension or stretching is dependent on the shape of the terrain — big hollows will require a longer stretch in order to keep the skis in contact with the snow.

From releasing the hold of the planted stick, the upper body follows a line to the inside of the turning arc. The basic neutral stance is resumed as the skis turn under the body, as a preparation ready to fold the legs and absorb the next terrain bump.

Important Pointers

Maintain a lowered body position with direct stick support until the skis have been turned downhill. A half-squat stance with the legs gives very good mechanical leverage to turn the skis. Plant the stick well downhill in order to get the maximum amount of support to aid pivotting of the skis.

Read the terrain so that the folding and stretching of the legs can be correctly synchronised with the shape of the terrain.

Compression Turns

Down sink, folding legs

Stick plant on bump crest

Pivot of legs and feet
to turn skis

F L

Stretching legs and
steering skis

Linked
Compression
Turns
over
bumps

79

Teaching Method — Compression Turns

This turning technique is intended specifically for skiing over bumps or mogulled slopes. Ideally the pupil should be at a good basic parallel standard, but the Basic Swing can be taught using the same folding and stretching leg movements.

The immediate change that faces the learner, is that of having to stay down in the folded position until after the skis have been turned. The tendency is to straighten up off the planted stick — unweighting action — and the Instructor should choose terrain and exercises that give the pupil the chance to feel the technical changes involved.

Introductory exercises should be chosen with regard to two important points. Firstly, that the skier should anticipate the terrain ahead and automatically bend and stretch the legs to maintain ski contact with the snow. In this way the skier's centre of gravity travels in a relatively horizontal line above the snow profile, neutralising the effect of the skis bouncing off the bumps.

Secondly, that the feel of swivelling the skis round under the feet to initiate the turn, must be learned. In this respect the mechanical leverage effect that is obtained from the folded leg position must be stressed.

In the folded leg position, the emphasis should be on equally weighting the boots — the whole foot taking the pressure distribution, although in an extreme squat there will be a tendency to sit back on the heels. To compensate for sitting back, the arms can be held further forward and to the side.

Support from the planted stick directly aids the turning of the legs and feet — a good grip on the stick out at arms length gives a longer period for support. Static exercises using the crest of a small hump should be demonstrated and tried by the pupils, in order to feel the pivotting action with the legs while leaning on the planted stick. A slight outward facing of the upper body on to the planted stick — anticipation — helps to release the legs and skis into the pivotting movement. Rolling the feet and skis off the edges to flatten and turn, followed by re-applying the opposite edges of the skis as the legs are extended.

Revise :—Basic Stance, Parallel Turns without unweighting using leg/feet turning action.

Terrain	In the ideal teaching situation, a series of evenly spaced ridges and hollows are constructed across the slope, in wave form. All exercises can be taught from straight running through to the final linked turns, on such a 'class room'. However, by careful selection, suitable bumps can be found that are not too close together, so that the pupil can attempt the exercises at a reasonably slow speed. On good snow conditions, all breakdown of movements can be practiced on smooth terrain.
Aids	Short Skis. Correctly selected terrain.
Exercises	1. Static. On hump pivotting skis with the feet around crest using stick support, with folded legs.
	2. Exercises using suitably even spaced bumps in wave form, to ski down fall-line, traverse across, fan swings into final turn. Feeling folding and extending of legs in correct relation to humps and hollows.
	3. Traverse across bumps, side-slipping down outside of bump by streching legs downhill, folding the legs on the crest as successive linked movements.
	4. Traverse across bumps, pivotting the skis on bumps and stretching the legs into small swings back in the traverse, in garland form.
	5. On smooth terrain. Narrow Plough in folded leg position to fall-line, closing the skis together with the leg extension. In garland form or by completed linked turns.
	6. On smooth terrain. Open stance parallel skis, simulating bend down — turn skis — stretch out legs into swing. In garland form or by complete linked turns.
	7. Moderate angled mogulled slope. Linked turns using crests to plant stick and turn, stretching out into the hollows. Varying the line downhill to ski more through the troughs of the bumps.
Common Faults	Extending the body upwards too early (as in up-weighting) instead of waiting in the folded position until the skis have turned downhill.
	Incorrect support from stick. Hold on to the stick until the skis have been steered around the crest.
	Having unequally weighted skis at the moment of pivotting on the bump. Results in crossed tips and snagged inner ski.

Exercises — Compression Turns

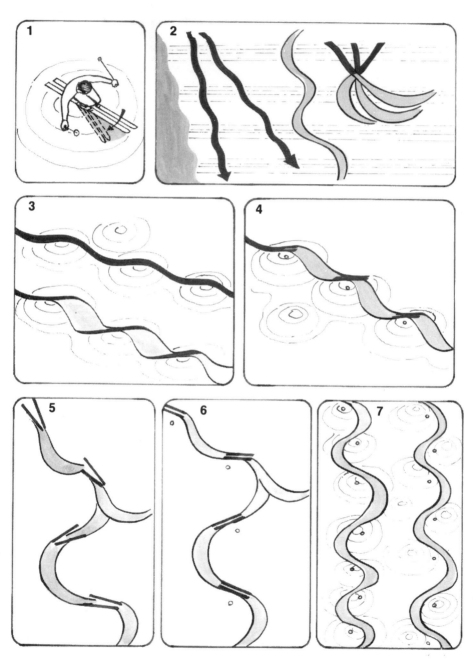

Not reading the terrain correctly. Turning movements are not smooth and fluent, to use the bumps correctly. Planting stick on downside of bump — stick skids off and rendered useless.

Correction Aids

Ensure the skiing speed is kept down by braking in the loose snow at the back of the mogul crest. Compression turns should be learned at a very controlled tempo, the skis should not be allowed to pick up speed.

Exercises on smooth terrain to practice middle to low folded stance, emphasising leg bend, leg turning, and stretch turning. From straight schuss in low squat to a quick turn across the line and stretch out legs into an emergency stop.

Snowplough turns in the middle stance, turning by leg/foot action only.

Basic Swings using middle plough stance, leg turning, stretching out to close skis into parallel swing.

NOTES

3

SKI TEACHING

Principles and Teaching Method
Artificial Slopes — Ski Teaching

SKI TEACHING

Teaching skiing, as with any other instruction situation, requires an understanding of the principles involved. Basically it is the ability to demonstrate and impart a technique or skill, with the result that the pupil learns and improves his/her own performance. In addition, the Instructor has the responsibility to the Class or Group for conduct and safety, while maintaining the highest personal and professional standards.

The essentials for good instruction are broadly:—

SAFETY — ENJOYMENT — LEARNING

Principles of Instruction

Personal qualities
Appearance important, the pupil immediately looks to the Instructor as an example. Friendliness, patience, enthusiasm and a readiness to communicate information are essential qualities.

Class management
Conduct the class safely with regard to their ability, the terrain, snow conditions and other skiers.

Observe the Courtesy Code for using lifts, runs and danger hazards.

Teaching Methods
Explain — speaking clearly and briefly, avoiding lengthy technical descriptions of technique.

Demonstrate precisely — the most important part of instruction.

Be able to demonstrate at all speeds, errors and at the class level.

Class Practice — the major part of a teaching session. Skiing is learned by doing, and not by standing still. Maximum activity by the group important, safely controlled.

Correction — the feedback from the pupil's performance.

Correct errors positively — analysis of main errors important.

Motivation — retain interest and avoid learning plateaux by varying the teaching pattern.

Use encouragement, different runs, aids, competitions, tests, etc.

Uncontrolled Factors
Age — older people are slower to learn than younger groups, and the teaching approach should be varied accordingly.

Sex — the obvious differences in physical strength between men and women should be taken into account. Psychological factors can also play an important part in the individual's learning capacity.

Physical ability — the build and general fitness of a person will dictate his/her performance level.

Snow conditions and weather — affect the speed of learning by the pupil.

Controlled Factors

Terrain — choosing the correct terrain for the standard of the group, and their safety.

Equipment — checking the correct size, type and condition of skis. Checking binding settings to pupil's standard, and adequately clothed.

Enjoyment and interest — directly associated by the method of teaching used, the motivation by the Instructor of the individual or whole group, and the amount of skiing practice achieved.

Application of the Teaching Method

Introduction procedure — check names, equipment, clothing, lift tickets and passes.

Revision Test Ski — test ski the group to assess their standard, in order to choose the next progression exercises. Be flexible in the use of the teaching progression, adapting it to suit the pupil's ability.

Explanation — stand in a position where all can see and hear, use simple terms briefly.

Demonstration — at the pupil's pace, away and towards the group, as necessary. Always demonstrate where and in which direction the pupil has to practice.

Class Practice — practice by the pupil, with the maximum activity of the group as a whole, forms the major part of class work.

Learning by imitation — following behind the Instructor is equally important to verbal instruction. Large groups increase the Instructor's supervision responsibility.

Fault Correction — choose different positions to view the pupil's performance. Analyse the main faults and give positive corrective advice or exercises, be ready to encourage the learner. Do not expect a perfect performance from the pupil, emphasise one correction point at a time.

The Instructor should have a full understanding of the cause of errors and the influencing factors, *e.g.*, pupil's physical limitations, emotional attitude, too advanced exercises, wrongly interpreted technical explanation, poor equipment, steepness of the slope, unsuitable snow conditions, weather — all should be taken into consideration to help the pupil progress.

General Conduct — the Instructor is responsible for the safe conduct of the group. Ensure that the class does not interfere or endanger them from other skiers, and that good order is maintained. Observe the Courtesy Code, and the correct procedure for the use of ski-lifts. Choose suitable terrain to aid the pupil's progress.

Vary the exercises and skiing to retain interest. Motivating the group to ensure enjoyment and successful improvement.

Instructor/Class — Factors

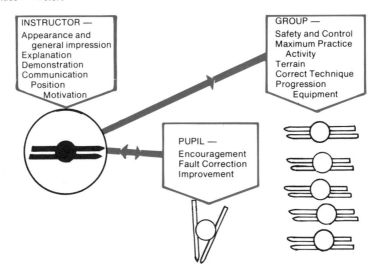

INSTRUCTOR —
Appearance and
  general impression
Explanation
Demonstration
Communication
  Position
  Motivation

GROUP —
Safety and Control
Maximum Practice
  Activity
Terrain
Correct Technique
Progression
  Equipment

PUPIL —
Encouragement
Fault Correction
Improvement

Instruction Position in Class Work

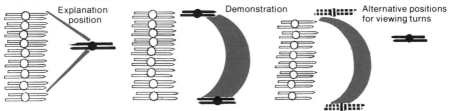

Explanation
position

Demonstration

Alternative positions
for viewing turns

Use of Terrain

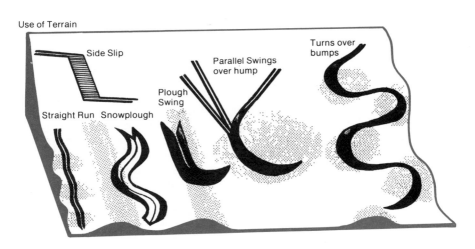

Side Slip

Turns over
bumps

Parallel Swings
over hump

Plough
Swing

Straight Run   Snowplough

ARTIFICIAL SLOPES — SKI TEACHING

The principles of teaching skiing are still applicable to the Instructor working on an Artificial Ski Slope. While Technique is basically that as applied to skiing on snow, some modification may be necessary. More angulation to hold the edge-grip and pressure to the lower ski, together with using a heel-hop for parallel skiing, are particular change examples.

The Teaching Method progression uses more skiing in the fall-line. While side-slipping can be taught, traversing may be difficult to teach, due to the size limitation of the slope. On small slopes the sessions will be orientated to exercise progression only, so to retain interest, the Instructor will have to use many varied exercises. On longer slopes, some limited running will be possible to add variety and practice to the session. Class sessions are shorter than those given on snow, therefore pupils must be given maximum activity in the time allowed. The Instructor will find that the duties extend beyond that of teaching skiing — the issue and fitting of equipment and general slope maintenance are part of the routine that involves working on an Artificial Slope.

Surface Materials

Several different types of materials have been manufactured to simulate the skiing properties of snow. All these materials have their own texture characteristic that affects sliding speed and edge control, together with certain wear depreciative effects. Design form of these materials are generally of fibre bristles or moulded plastic stalks, made up into mats or moulded shapes that link up to cover the slope.

The skis slide directly over the material when running straight, having a slower speed comparison to snow, but becoming faster when damp. Edge control (turning, side-slipping, stopping) depends on the resilience of the bristle forms to resist against the edging action of the skis. Excessive wear of the materials, especially as the slope angle increases, can have a marked effect on edge control.

It is essential that the Ski Instructor is aware of the limitations of the slope material on which instruction is to be given.

Equipment

Shorter length skis are used generally on Artificial Slopes, and as these are easier to turn, the Instructor should bear in mind any modification of the teaching method that may be necessary.
Ski Sticks are blunt ended and without snow-baskets to avoid snagging on the slope.

Class Management and Safety

Because of the confines of an artificial slope, the Instructor has a special responsibility for the safety of students while conducting a ski class. This is particularly applicable to slopes that are not served by mechanical uplift and pupils have to side-step back uphill on the slope surface. On slopes that have a limited running area, the Instructor must ensure that students climb up at the side to avoid collision with skiers running down the slope. The Instructor should limit the height at which the student can safely ski down the slope, ensuring that they clear the bottom of the slope quickly and climb back up again in an orderly manner.
Falling down is still part of skiing, even on an artificial slope, and as the material is harder to fall on than snow, the Instructor must demonstrate the correct way to fall. Most important the hands should not be stretched out to arrest a fall, as thumbs and fingers can be injured when caught in the spaces between the material. Legs and arms should be adequately covered to avoid friction burns.
The design of the slope and the maintenance of the material used can be a possible safety hazard, also ski slope materials become worn with use. Carefully inspect the slope periodically to ensure that no projections, loose edges or foreign bodies are on the matting that may snag the skis.
A complete First-Aid Kit should be available close at hand.
The additional safety points then to be considered when working on an Artificial Slope are briefly:—
1. Familiarise as to the best use for teaching progression and conditon of the slope.
2. Check students' clothing, mitts, ski equipment.
3. Demonstrate and have the pupils practise the correct way to fall.
4. Students must be controlled in their movements up and down the slope to avoid collision.

NOTES

4

CROSS-COUNTRY SKIING

Proficiency Tests
Pre-Ski Exercises

CROSS-COUNTRY SKIING

Increased interest in Cross-Country Skiing may involve the Ski Instructor in this branch of ski sport. The technique and test/instructor certificates outlined are for basic reference only, full particulars should be obtained from the BASI — Nordic Section.

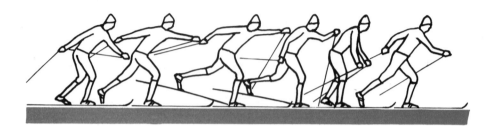

Two Phase Step (Diagonal Gait)

The basic step, using the normal walking action of opposite arm and leg swing, but extended to 'kick' down and glide forward with the legs. The arm and stick are swung forward to give the maximum amount of push off the stick. Rhythm and co-ordination of movements, with the minimum of twisting or up/down body motion, is essential for efficient striding with the least effort.

Double Sticking, or Punting

Using the sticks to push and glide forward is used as a combination with the Two Phase Step, to produce a variety of steps. On easy gradients, double sticking gives forward speed without using the step action. Reach well forward to obtain the maximum push down and follow through with the arms.

Uphill Climbing Step

Using the Two Phase Step, the stride is shortened to allow for a long 'kick' down or press on the gripping ski to the snow. On steeper slopes the step can be made in series of diagonal tacks, or by using the Herringbone Step.

Turning

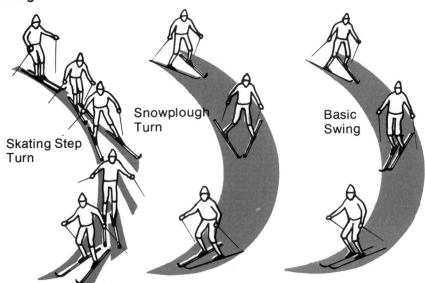

Skating Step Turn

Snowplough Turn

Basic Swing

Skating Step Turn — By stepping out and gliding onto the ski in the direction of the turn, speed can be maintained when turning on the flat and easy slopes.

Snowplough and Basic Swing Turns — Where the slopes are steeper then the Snowplough is used, finishing to skid parallel if possible as in the Basic Swing. The technique is standard, but requires more pressure on the heels — apropos, loose heel bindings.

Equipment	The Nordic ski is longer, narrower and lighter than the Alpine ski. Racing Cross-Country skis are narrow and very light, skis for more general touring are wider, with edges, made of wood or G.R.P. Correct length of skis are from 20 to 30 cms above ths skier's height, stick length 30-35 cms below the skier's height.
Waxing	Correct waxing technique is an important aspect of Nordic skiing. Waxes are chosen according to the snow condition and temperature, requiring that the ski will 'grip' when the kick-down is made and then glide forward on the stride. Klister waxes are soft and sticky in tubes, Stick waxes are hard and rubbed on the ski. As a general rule, if a ski slips back, use a softer or thicker layer of wax. If snow sticks to the ski, use a harder stick wax. Candidates for the Cross-Country Ski Instructor's Certificate require to have a full knowledge of the technique and principles of waxing.

British Cross-Country Ski Tests

The proficiency Tests are administered by the British Ski Federation Nordic Section.

Bronze (One Star) Test Elementary skiing, open to all British skiers of any age. Taken on snow or suitably laid artificial ski track.
1. (a) Two Phase, Alternating, Diagonal Step with and without sticks.
   (b) Double Sticking, or Punting.
   (c) Herringbone Climbing.
   (d) Downhill direct descent.
   (e) Snowplough Stop.
   (f) Kick Turn.
2. Either, on snow — 5 Km. conducted tour.

Silver (Two Star) Test Intermediate skiing. Taken on snow, and having basic knowledge of waxing. Not a racing test, but at a level for any competent cross-country skier. Must have passed the Bronze Test.
1. (a) Four Phase or Swedish step.
   (b) Double stick push with alternate leg kick.
   (c) Skating turns to left and right.
   (d) Traverse climb with three turns.
   (e) Downhill traverse in both directions, step up to stop.
   (f) Four linked Snowplough Turns.

2. On snow, run of 8 Km. in 55 mins., on prepared course or tour.
3. Explain differences in running waxes and basic principles.

Gold (Three Star) Test Advanced skiing. Requires a high standard of competence, must have passed the Silver Test.
1. *(a)* Three Phase running or single arm resting.
   (b) Double sticking with two steps.
   (c) Five phase running.
   (d) Four linked Stem turns.
   (e) Downhill skating turns through 90°, both directions.
2. Run 15 Kms. in 63 mins., on a prepared track.
3. Demonstrate waxing new skis.
4. Explain how to fit binding.

British Nordic Ski Instructors' Certificates

The training and grading for Nordic Ski Instructors is administered by the British Association of Ski Instructors.

Any British subject over the age of 18 years, may offer themselves for examination.

The grades of Instructor are:—

Grade III Basic Instructor, teaching the basic techniques of cross-country skiing to beginners.

Grade II Advanced Instructor, with ability to conduct advanced cross-country ski training and courses.

Grade I International Level Instructor, with the ability to set race courses in accordance with F.I.S. rules.
Organise race meetings and advise on race training and equipment.

Examination Syllabi
Grade III
1. Candidate must have passed the Bronze Cross-Country Test.
2. Demonstrate and teach the following:—
   (a) Two Phase Alternating step, Diagonal gait, with and without sticks.
   (b) Punting, or Double Sticking.
   (c) Herringbone Climbing.
   (d) Direct Downhill Descents.
   (e) Snowplough Stops.
   (f) Snowplough Turns to right and left.
   (g) Kick Turns to right and left.
3. Technical knowledge:—
   (a) Basic principles of waxing.
   (b) Be capable of fitting cross-country ski bindings.
   (c) Advise pupils on ski and stick lengths required.

**Grade II
Certificate**

1. Candidate must have passed the Silver Cross-Country Test, and hold a valid Grade III Instructor's Certificate.
2. Demonstrate and teach the following:—
   (a) Three Phase alternating step.
   (b) Four Phase alternating step.
   (c) Double sticking.
   (d) Double sticking with one stride.
   (e) Double sticking with two strides.
   (f) Five Phase alternating step.
   (g) Skating.
   (h) Skating turns.
   (i) Direct Climbs.
   (j) Side Slipping.
3. Technical knowledge:—
   (a) Demonstrate the principles of waxing.
   (b) Training — Aerobic, Anaerobic, Muscular, Endurance, Duration.
   (c) Different types of skis and bindings, and fitting them.
   (d) Prepare an annual training programme.
   (e) F.I.S. Rules.

**Grade I
Certificate**

1. Candidate must hold a valid Grade III Cross-Country Instructor's Certificate.
2. Technical Knowledge:—
   (a) Detailed knowledge of the F.I.S. Rules for Cross-Country Racing and course setting.
   (b) Ability to set a Championship Cross-Country ski race course for men or women.
   (c) General knowledge of different types of equipment for touring and racing, and advise on the selection of equipment for all types of cross-country skiing.

Full current details apply to:—

BASI
Inverdruie Visitor Centre
Rothiemurchus
Aviemore
Inverness-shire PH22 1QH

SKIING PROFICIENCY TEST

The British Ski Federation and Scottish National Ski Council administer the following Proficiency Tests. Registered qualified Ski Instructors are required to assist in the examination of these tests.

British Junior Alpine Ski Tests
(open to skiers under the age of 18 years)

ONE STAR TEST
Test can be taken on snow or artificial ski slopes in Great Britain, Alps, Norway, etc.
1. Climbing. Side step.
2. Descent. Straight schuss.
3. Snowplough glide descent to a controlled stop.
4. Diagonal traverse to left and right.
5. A linked consecutive right and left snowplough or basic swing turns.
6. Ski Educational questions.

TWO STAR TEST
Test can be taken on snow or artificial ski slopes in Great Britain, Alps, Norway, etc.
1. Direct controlled side-slip of at least 5 metres in either direction.
2. Diagonal controlled side-slip of at least 5 metres in either direction.
3. 4-6 consecutive basic swing or parallel turns.
4. Non-stop no falls descent through at least 6 open gates.
5. Swing to the slope to a stop from a steep traverse to left and right.
6. Ski Educational questions.

THREE STAR TEST
Advanced Skiing Test
Candidates must ski to a good parallel standard. Tests can be taken on approved artificial slopes (over 130ft. long) or on snow in Great Britain, Alps, Norway, etc. Candidates must hold 2-Star test badge.
1. 4 long continuous parallel turns with sticks.
2. 4 long continuous parallel turns without sticks.
3. 8-12 linked continuous short parallel turns.
4. 8-12 single gate slalom run down slope. No fall descent through the gates.
5. Ski Educational questions.

or, Racing Test
Test can only be taken on snow. Candidates must hold a 2-Star test badge.
1. At least 30 gate slalom. Candidates must be within 30% of the vorlaufer's time.
2. No falls non-stop downhill run of at least 300 metres on a piste. Candidates must be within 30% of the vorlaufer's time.
3. Ski Educational questions.

Full details of these tests, assessment forms, ski education pamphlet, etc. can be obtained from the National Offices — B.S.F. and S.N.S.C. — addresses are at the end of this book.

PRE-SKI EXERCISES AND TRAINING

Skiing requires good muscle tone, stamina and breathing control. The legs, back, shoulders and arms are areas where muscle tone and strength is important. The exercises suggested here form part of an overall training plan, basically to ensure that a fit skier is a safe skier. Fitness is the best protection against injury. Always warm up by running on the spot for a few minutes.

1. **Step-ups —**
Stepping up and down to a box, bench or stairs (leg, lungs).

2. **Press-ups —**
Support on arms, lowering and pressing back up, from the floor or chairseat (arms, shoulders).

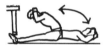

3. **Trunk Curls —**
Lying on floor, toes hooked under a support. Hands behind head, sit and curl forward from waist (back, stomach).

4. **Squat Thrusts —**
From low crouch, hands on floor. Hop legs back into fully stretched out position. Jump forward into crouch (legs, arms).

5. **Back Curls —**
From lying face down, lift head and legs off floor (back).

6. **Arm Dips —**
From support between two chairs or bars. Bend arms and lift body back up again without feet touching floor (arms).

7. **Squat Jumps —**
From the crouch squat position, hop up and down as high as possible. Hop forward and to the side (legs).

8. **Wall Sit —**
Sitting against wall, thighs at right angle to lower legs (legs).

Exercises 1 to 7 are a series in circuit training.

Find the starting level at each exercise by trying for the maximum and then reducing to half the number. Alternatively take a time limit, e.g. 20 seconds for each exercise. Increase with the level of fitness attained.

Warm down each session by flexing exercises, arms and legs circling, head circling, toe touching, side presses, loose jogging, deep breathing.

Other Conditioning Training

Cross-country running — jogging over undulating terrain.

Cycling — time a circuit to check performance (10 miles in 30 minutes — good).

Rope skipping — Build up intervals of fast and medium step skips, from $1\frac{1}{2}$ mins.

On snow — Short swings and hop checks from side to side, with side stepping back up the slope! Make a target of a set number with each run, e.g. 20, and increase in 10's.

NOTES

5
MOUNTAIN SAFETY

Skiers Code

Snowcraft

Avalanche Evaluation

First Aid

Mountain Safety Appendix

SAFETY IN THE MOUNTAINS

Skiing, like most other exhilerating sports, has an element of risk attached to its participation. It is important for the ski instructor, with responsibility for the safety of his class, to have a respect for these dangers, by observing the simple rules, recognising the danger situations and the necessary precautions and actions to avoid becoming involved in an accident. Hazards occur in all facets of skiing — piste 'traffic', snow avalanches, bad weather, wrong route finding, poor ski technique, in fact all the aspects confronting the winter mountain traveller. The space limitations of this manual make it only possible to outline briefly these dangers and the immediate action to be taken. For more detailed information and in conjunction with the Ski Instructor Course lectures, candidates are advised to read the publications referred to in the Mountain Safety Appendix at the end of this Section.

Skiers Courtesy Code

To ensure safety on the piste and have courtesy to other skiing traffic the FIS have laid down the following rules:

1. Respect — a skier's conduct should in no way prejudice or endanger others.
2. Speed and Control — a skier must ski in control at all times. Be able to stop when necessary and avoid other skiers.
3. Slower skiers always have the right of way.
4. Overtaking — the overtaking skier must give a wide margin to the overtaken skier and not impede the slower skier's path. If necessary give an audible warning of approach from behind.
5. Stopping — a skier must avoid, whenever possible, stopping in the middle of the piste or narrow trail. Move to the side, as soon as possible, to ensure the safety and free passage of other skiers.
6. Starting off — before starting off or when crossing another track, look first to make sure the way is clear of other skiers.
7. Walking or climbing — when it is necessary to walk or climb near a piste use only the side of the trail, never walk or climb in the middle.
8. Intersections — the skier entering a main slope from an intersecting piste, shall give way to skiers on the main slope.

9. Skiers approaching each other on opposite traverses should pass to the left. Keep left is the rule.
10. Piste Signs — observe and obey all signs placed to control downhill skiing and the use of lifts. At all times co-operate with lift staff and the Ski Patrol.
11. Accidents — stop and assist if necessary, give identity particulars if required.

   To enjoy skiing, it is necessary to have a respect for other skiers. Give the learner skiers the benefit of the doubt, leave plenty of room for them to manoeuvre in safety. Use ski lifts correctly, wait in turn and do not mal-use the lift equipment. If you fall, fill in any holes made in the snow before moving off. Use a retaining means on your skis to prevent a run-away ski. Stop skiing when tired — at all times be courteous.

INTERNATIONAL SKI RUN, PISTE SIGNS

Caution Crossways Ski Lift crossing SOS Telephone First-Aid Post

Steeper slope Run narrows Bumps & Hollows Run crosses road traffic Through Gangway

Turn Junction Change of direction Piste or Run marker

Snowcraft

Snow undergoes a continual change once it falls. Some of these changes can effect adversely the snow's skiable conditions, others affect the stable attitude of the snow that can lead to avalanche conditions, which are outlined later. Surface snow conditions that may have given reasonable skiing, can be quickly turned into unpleasant, difficult snow on which to ski. This can be due to weather change, wind, sun, rain, frost, new snowfall and many other factors. In the interests of safety and the responsibility of his class, the ski instructor should be able to recognise these dangerous conditions, requiring extreme caution to avoid possible accident or injury occurring when attempting to ski down.

**Difficult skiable
snow:—**

Breakable crust

Formed by the snow surface melting and freezing to form a crust that will not support the skier's weight. The skis break through this crust making it impossible to turn in the normal manner, resorting to traverses and kick turns as a means of descent. Slopes facing directly towards the sun are prone to crust formation especially in the late afternoon.

Wind eroded snow

Formed into waves of hard snow by high winds. Requires extreme care to avoid hooking a tip into the wave crests, again the safest way to negotiate these passages is by slow traverses at a shallow angle line.

Heavy wet snow

The result of thaw conditions producing deep mush snow. Apart from the skis sliding slower, the heavy snow traps the ski and requires more power to turn the skis. Care has to be exercised when stemming or ploughing to avoid the ski digging in or blocking the effort of turning.

Hard frozen, icy snow

Conditions that may occur on unpisted snow slopes especially facing directly into the sun, after extremes of melt and frost; also occurs on pistes that have been polished by skiing use. On unpisted slopes the surface usually has a slight grain on which it is possible to get some edge purchase but steep slopes should be avoided. On the piste the surface is much smoother making edging difficult on steeper pitches in particular. Choose a lie that takes in all the flatter sections and look for any patches of loose snow, side-slip down the sides of the piste where there may be a better surface grip.

Wind slab

Formed by accumulations of snow masses, usually on lee slopes after storm conditions. When skiied on, the snow breaks away into slabs and chunks making turning control difficult. On steeper slopes, a simple traverse line is hard to hold as the skis continually break away, caution has also to be observed for possible avalanche, as described later.

Deep rutted frozen snow

Usually occurs in the spring after a hot day of skiing on coarse granular snow. As the sun goes down, freezing sets in immediately, turning the ski tracks into hard lumps that catch the edge of the ski. Choose a careful line to avoid the worst patches.

Deep powdered snow on mogulled piste

When deep new snow covers the humps and hollows of a well used piste, the danger lies in hitting the hard crests of the moguls underneath the snow cover. Ski very cautiously and at a very controlled speed in order to avoid being thrown when hitting a submerged crest.

Leaving the piste

In new snow cover over an old narrow piste base, beware of underlying rocks and other obstacles at the sides that are only thinly covered and can cause damage to both ski and skier! When there has been a new wet snow cover, allow the skis to track straight when running off the piste into untracked snow. Allow for any deceleration effect on the skis and 'feel' the snow before attempting to turn.

AVALANCHE EVALUATION

Avalanches are a mountain hazard that must be considered seriously by the ski Instructor. Recognising potentially dangerous slopes, snow conditions and precautions taken to avoid being involved in an avalanche, should be part of every skier's knowledge. All Instructors should be acquainted with the Rescue facilities in their area.

The full study of avalanches and why they occur, is a very complex subject, and only a general outline can be given here.

Reference publications are listed in the Bibliography for more comprehensive information.

Snow crystal formation

Snow Crystal Metamorphosis

Snow crystals form through atmospheric conditions giving water vapour precipitation below freezing temperature. They fall as a variety of shapes, from the fine granule of very cold conditions to large wet flakes at near freezing point. Once fallen as part of the snow cover, the crystals begin a process of change in their form that can occur very quickly or take several weeks, depending on the influencing conditions of weather and temperature.

Snow layer structure

Snow Layers — differences between layers may cause unstable conditions

Each snow fall forms a new layer of snow that has its own characteristic of crystal change. Within the general snow cover these layers of snow and their different physical characteristics to one another, affect the possibility of avalanche — given the shape and angle of the terrain.

Adjacent snow layers may not stick to one another, or the whole mass of snow due to its weight are factors that make slopes unstable.

Destructive Metamorphism — The crystals lose their shape into compact rounded granules, and eventually the snow layer settles. In cold temperatures this is powder snow, and is unstable until time and weather have consolidated the layer.

Constructive Metamorphism — Occurs wiithin the layers of snow, due to temperature changes from layer to layer. Water vapour from the warmer lower levels moves upwards and can re-sublime on crystals at a suitable juncture. These crystals grow into hexagonal cup shapes that form an unstable layer within the snow cover.

Surface Hoar — Over a period of cold, clear nights, crystals may form on the snow surface when subject to suitable water vapour conditions. These are the leaf-like crystals of surface hoar, and after subsequent snowfalls may form a fragile, unstable layer in the snow cover.

Mechanical Properties of Snow — Snow is a plastic material of elastic and viscous properties. Under gravity it will 'creep' downhill, setting up tensile stresses within the layer.

Snow falling under strong wind conditions — wind packed snow — increases the hardness and brittleness of the snow structure.

Avalanche Types

Loose snow avalanches — Start from a single point, and usually involve only the top surface strata of the snow cover.

Dry new snow avalanches occur after new snowfall, but are not particularly dangerous unless they become airborne when the speed accelerates rapidly producing lethal shock waves.

Wet snow avalanches occur as the snow melts, usually in the Spring, moving slowly in a heavy mass of solid, wet snow.

Slab avalanches — are responsible for the majority of accidents. Wind packed snow into a slab layer form an unstable layer. The adhesion of the snow to the top and sides of the slope can be so critical that only the slightest upset in this balance is required to fracture the snow. Slab avalanches break away in a large area of blocks, usually on open slopes. This type of avalanche is not only a particular risk in Alpine terrain, but also encountered in Scottish skiing due to high winds building up slab snow on sheltered lee slopes.

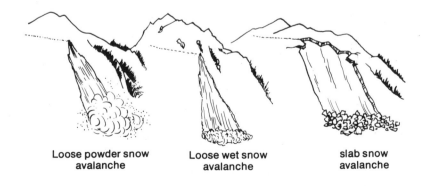

Loose powder snow   Loose wet snow   slab snow
avalanche   avalanche   avalanche

Precautions

The best warning of avalanche danger is avalanches! — and most accidents are caused by the victims they bury!

Greatest danger is during and after heavy winter storms. Greater the depth of snow, the more likely slides will occur. Look for signs of slab snow conditions, a ski track is a deadly means of providing a fracture line.

Avoid open steep slopes, especially if convex and smooth terrain.

Keep as high as possible, or on ridges, staying on broken ground with rocks, trees and hollows that tend to anchor the snow better.

Avoid cornices and slopes ending in a steep drop. Gullies are dangerous, where even a small slide can bury the victims deeply.

Cross dangerous ground one at a time quickly. If necessary go on foot than on ski, and straight down rather than traverse.

Carry and use an avalanche cord. Check with local expert knowledge for known avalanche slopes, or factors affecting avalanche risk.

Observe all avalanche danger signs and do not ski on closed routes.

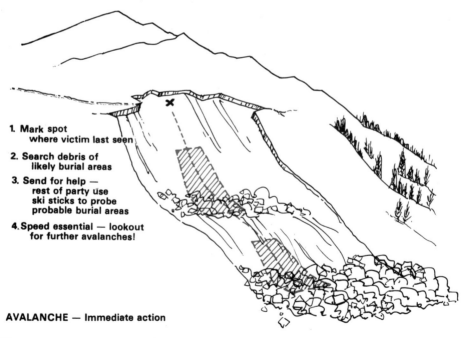

1. **Mark spot** where victim last seen

2. **Search debris of** likely burial areas

3. **Send for help —** rest of party use ski sticks to probe probable burial areas

4. **Speed essential — lookout** for further avalanches!

AVALANCHE — Immediate action

Action if caught in an avalanche

If on skis and possible to ski away — do so!
Throw off skis, sticks and rucksack — look for the best way of escape.
Swim on surface, keep mouth shut, as the avalanche comes to rest try to create a space for face and chest. Push anything through to the surface! Try not to panic! Shout for help.

Search and rescue action

Mark the last known positions of victims.
Search whole area for any signs, ensuring no further avalanche danger exists — keep silent!
Send for help immediately with precise details of the location.
Speed is vital, use reversed ski sticks to make a superficial sounding.
Apply first-aid to victim when located — clear air passages immediately.

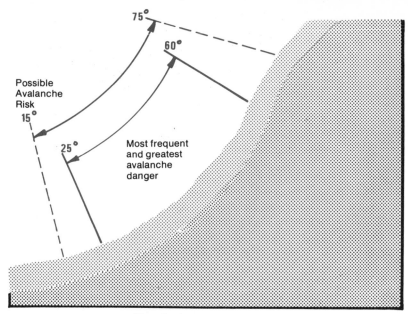

Possible
Avalanche
Risk
15°

75°

60°

25°

Most frequent
and greatest
avalanche
danger

Slope Angles — Avalanche Risk

**Potentially
dangerous slopes**

Any slope at a critical slide angle (over 15°) and covered with unstable snow, is an avalanche risk — whether it is in a remote mountain area or next to a ski-run or lift. Smooth ground, without any natural break-up features such as rocks or trees, and if convex shaped, is potentially dangerous terrain. Steep gullies and open slopes are natural avalanche paths.

FIRST-AID

In the event of injury to a skier, the Instructor or Party Leader should take these immediate actions.

1. Re-group the rest of the class or party together, in the case of inexperienced skiers, take off their skis to keep them safely under control and avoid further accidents happening.

2. Give immediate assistance to the injured person. Place crossed skis above the person as a protection and warning to others. Make the person comfortable and warm by placing ski jackets, gloves, etc., around and underneath the body. Administer first-aid, keep the person calm, look to breathing, arrest any bleeding and easing of pain. Immobolise and avoid excessive movement of limbs in cases of suspected fracture. Do not remove boots or offer alcoholic drink.

3. Send for the Ski Patrol. Despatch only a competent skier for help, with details of the exact location of the accident. With beginner groups, send someone on foot only. The instructor must stay with the injured person, ensuring that he/she is kept warm to avoid chilling and possible shock.

4. If no help is immediately available, it may be necessary to apply some method of emergency splinting to the injured limbs. In extreme emergency it may be necessary to construct a makeshift sledge in order to facilitate the safe evacuation of the injured person.

   Reference to mountain rescue procedure will be found in the Mountain Safety Appendix. It is also recommended that an Instructor should possess the Elementary First-Aid Certificate.

General Precautions

To prevent injury or accident, certain precautions should be taken.

Ensure that everyone has adequate warm and windproof clothing, remember Scottish weather in particular can be of Arctic severity. Keep close to lift lines in 'white-out' or poor visibility. Never ski off alone away from the piste, leave full information of intended route and times. Check weather conditions. Take out contingency insurance cover such as offered by the Scottish National Ski Council.

113

Carry in a waist bag for piste skiing:—
Spare goggles or glasses, suncream, spare safety straps, triangular and crepe bandages, safety pins, tin of 'bandaids', multi-purpose knife (screw-driver, etc.), cord or laces.

For touring away from the piste carry:—
Map, compass, whistle, matches, wire-splint, torch, emergency rations, extra windproof over-clothing, spare blanket or polythene bag for emergency bivouac.

CROSSED SKIS for warning

Apply first-aid and make person comfortable

Keep group together to provide shelter and warmth

Pack spare clothing underneath person

Pad out improvised splints

Send for Ski Patrol

ACCIDENT PROCEDURE

MOUNTAIN SAFETY APPENDIX

Ski Instructor Course syllabus includes coverage of the following additional mountain safety subjects. The relevant information can be obtained from the publications listed in the Bibliography at the end of this book.

Weather —
Interpretation of the weather map. Major cloud forms and associated weather developments. Sources of weather information — radio, TV, newspapers, met. stations.

Navigation —
Map reading, use of compass, calculating speed of movement, methods of obtaining bearings, natural wayfinding (use of sun and stars), methods of teaching simple map and compass work to beginners.

Route Planning, Ski Touring —
Choice of route. Preparation of route cards. Escape routes, bad weather alternatives. Sources of rescue aid — telephones, Moutain Rescue Posts, Ski Patrol, etc. Party management, leader, tailman.

Clothing and equipment
Personal clothing required for mountain skiing in all weather conditions. Effects of wind, temperature, humidity when using various clothing materials. Care and maintenance. Basic principles of insulation, values of wind and waterproofing.

First-Aid and Accident Procedure —
Procedure in the event of an accident. Methods of winter search and evacuation. Improvised rescue equipment rope seats and stretchers, construction of ski sleds and stretchers.

Emergency Procedure —
Emergency bivouacs equipment and procedure. Construction of snow holes and emergency shelters.

Special Mountain Hazards —
Recognition of signs, symptoms, prevention and treatment of — Exposure, Frostbite, Heat Exhaustion and Sunburn, and Snow Blindness.

NOTES

6

SKI EQUIPMENT

Skis — Design and Types
Bindings and Boots
Care and Maintenance

SKI EQUIPMENT — Design and Function.

SKIS

The design and manufacture of skis has changed greatly since the pre-war wooden skis. They are now made from many different materials — metal, fibreglass, plastic laminates, etc., under strict quality control conditions. The modern ski has undergone intensive technological research in order to meet top racing performance and the expansion of a skiing market. To perform satisfactorily a ski must be able to stay on track and also turn easily, responding to the controlling movements of edge setting, displacement of the centre of gravity such as weighting or unweighting, or forward and backward shifting, as well as more or less emphasised side-slipping phases of single or both skis. If these requirements are met, then a ski will feel to turn easily and not be unstable or chatter, the edges will hold to carve and make round smooth turns, at the same time, it will have stability to track straight without any tendency to wander. Apart from the skis tracking performance, the manufacturer has to ensure that the ski will wear well, having sufficient resistance to rupture according to the quality and and that it is attractively finished for marketing. The characteristics determining the performance of a ski are defined as follows:—

Length and size — size standard measured in centimetres, usually in steps of 5 cms. The length and width of skis determines the tracking qualities, greater length inversely affects turning ability.

Camber — The built-in arch along the ski length. This helps to distribute the skier's weight and is usually in direct proportion of the flexibility.

Bending flex — The degree of flex measured along the length of the ski. A ski can have different degrees of bending flex at the forepart, centre and heel according to the design requirements. Lightweight skiers should use a softer flex ski than heavier built skiers. Advanced skiing turns require a stiffer heel than the forepart of the ski.

Torsional stiffness — The twisting force along the ski. The more a ski resists torsion the more it bites into the snow, but can lead to chatter and be harder to turn through moguls.

Damping — The ability of a ski to absorb flexing and vibrations set up when edging or skiing through bumpy terrain.

TYPES OF SKIS.

Slalom Ski

This ski is designed with a narrow waist giving more side camber and a stiffer flex, so that the ski has good edge bite and turning ability.

Downhill Ski

Speed and straight tracking is the essential requirements of a downhill ski. They are designed with minimum side camber, are usually longer and the forepart has a softer flex to absorb high speed shocks.

Giant Slalom Ski

Designed to fill the needs in between the extremes of slalom and downhill skiing. Waisting and flex are of medium dimensions and rating.

Recreational Ski

Most recreational skis are basically giant slalom skis in size and dimensions but vary in flex rating according to the quality and requirement. For example, deep snow skis are a softer overall flex than a ski used on hard pisted snow.

Short & Compact Skis

Specifically designed to aid learner skiers into parallel skiing through graduated lengths from 100 cms. to 180 cms. approx. High performance short and compact skis 160-190 cms. are easier to turn than normal length skis and are used for advanced and acrobatic skiing.

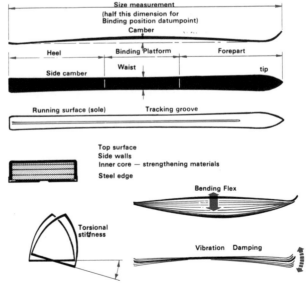

SKI BINDINGS.

In the search for safer skiing, bindings have been, and will continue to be, subject to detailed research. The primary functions are to hold the boot and foot in place whilst performing normal skiing movements but at the same time, allow the boot to release if the skier falls awkwardly or imposes a loading on the foot or leg where injury may occur. There are a multiplicity of binding designs having various mechanical release and adjustment means. All release bindings are only as safe as the correct adjustment and maintenance allows.

Binding placement

The position of the binding on the ski is relative to the boot size and the specific use of the ski. The mid-point of the ski is generally used as the datum for placing the toe-piece. This mark is measured at halfway from the projected tip to heel length. The toe end of the boot is positioned from this mark, so that the ball of the foot is over the centre of the ski's running surface. On slalom skis, the mounting is placed at least 1 cm. forward and on downhill skis, the mounting is placed 1 cm. rearwards. For larger size boots, size 10 upwards move the binding approx. 1 cm. towards the tip, and for boots size 6 and smaller move the bindings at least 1 cm rearwards.

BOOTS

The important function of correct fitting boots is to give a positive support to the foot when edging the skis, or when shifting the weight pressure forward or backwards on the ski. Modern boots are designed to provide a stiff lateral support to the ankle and prevent the heel from lifting when pressing the knees forward or sinking back in a deep squat position. Stiff outer boot shells of leather or moulded plastic materials ensure that there is an immediate response to leg action, while various methods of inner padding are used to make the foot snug and comfortable.

Ski Sticks

Ski sticks are designed to give a comfortable responsive swing, retaining strength with lightness. The length of a stick is measured by taking hold of the stick upside down and grasping the shaft below the basket. The hand should be at elbow height, with the forearm horizontal.

Equipment Safety Checks

Check that bindings are well lubricated and skis are kept in good order.
Check the release settings are correctly adjusted before skiing.
Keep the ski boot sole and anti-friction plates clean.
Inspect safety retaining straps and braking devices for serviceable condition.

Bindings — Release Direction

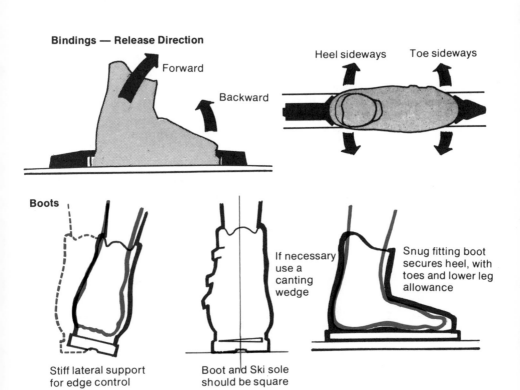

Forward

Backward

Heel sideways

Toe sideways

Boots

Stiff lateral support for edge control

Boot and Ski sole should be square

If necessary use a canting wedge

Snug fitting boot secures heel, with toes and lower leg allowance

CARE AND MAINTENANCE OF SKIS.

Before undertaking any routine repair work, it is necessary to carefully inspect the skis, assessing the general condition and amount of servicing required. Always clean and dry the skis, check the bottoms for scratches, gouges and 'railing' wear at the joint between sole and steel edge. Carefully check with a metal straight edge the flatness of the ski bottom, finally examine the steel edges for sharpness, burrs and that the sides form a perfect right angle.

Sole Repair

Clean away all traces of wax from the damaged area, then fill in with melted drip from the correct sole material repair candle stick. Hold the stick close to the area until filled proud of the running surface. Allow to cool, then carefully trim off flush with a chisel or sharp bladed tool. Check that no small holes remain in the repair, then finish off by rubbing down with fine emery paper wrapped round a sanding block.

Edge Filing

Check that the bottom of the skis is uniformly flat — the edge of a metal wax scraper placed across the ski will show any wear in the sole centre. Concave soles will require flat filing, do this by holding a 10 inch mill bastard file diagonally across the skis. Secure the ski, sole upwards, file from the tip to heel with long, light strokes, keeping even pressure on both edges. Ski edges should be sharpened to give a smooth clean edge at a perfect 90° angle, tested by drawing the finger nail across the edge to take off a light nail shaving. Secure the ski on its side and holding the file square to the side, work from tip to heel in light steady strokes of about 6 – 8 inches evenly overlapping to avoid a wavy edge line. Hone-up the edge on the running surface in the same way. Finally polish away any file striations or burrs with emery paper or a sharpening stone. The edges on the shovel of the ski may require dulling down a little to avoid the tips hooking into the snow. Wipe off the cuttings from the ski and keep the file clean throughout the operation.

Waxing

To obtain the best sliding performance of a ski, waxing is still necessary. All new skis should have a wax application before use and continual waxing helps to protect and minimise wear on the ski sole. Hot wax application ensures a strong bond to the polyethylene base. Choose a wax according to the snow conditions, blue for regular cold snow, green for cold power, red for warmer snow, mixing the waxes for intermediate snow conditions. Add paraffin wax to widen the particular wax temperature range. Scrape off old wax first if preparation of the edges and soles unnecessary.

Painting method

Heat the wax in a pot or old saucepan until it just gives off a light smoke. Use a thin section brush at least 1½" wide, dip into the wax and press against the pot side to remove air bubbles. Begin at the ski heel and paint on wax in approx. 12" strokes, overlapping each stroke to produce steps. Shorten the wax strokes to produce more steps for wet snow conditions, this reduces the suction of the sole on to the snow surface. Paint down both sides of the ski sole from the centre groove in equal strokes. Scrape the whole sole with the metal scraper to a smooth layer of wax, removing wax from the centre groove and edges with a suitably shaped plastic or wood scraper. Finally polish the bottoms with a clean cloth until they shine. Insert paper between the ski tips and heels for carrying to the lifts.

Ironing Method

Lay skis side by side, soles upwards and supported at tips and heels. Set the iron at medium heat and press edge of wax against iron held point downwards over the sole. Keeping the iron just clear of the surface, drip the melted wax in a stream along the sole on both sides of the groove. Smooth out the wax with the iron held flat, moving all the time to prevent the wax bubbling and overheating the polyethylene sole material. Scrape and finish as outlined in the previous painting method.

Edge Filing

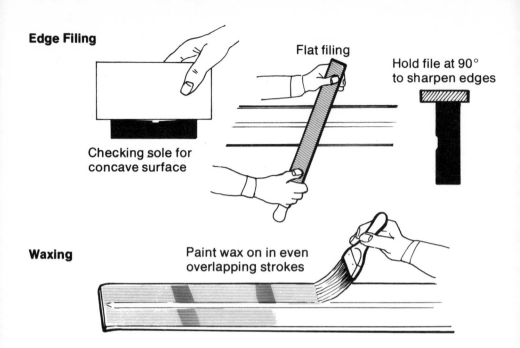

Checking sole for concave surface

Flat filing

Hold file at 90° to sharpen edges

Waxing

Paint wax on in even overlapping strokes

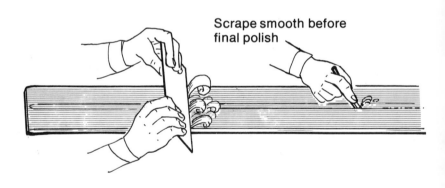

Scrape smooth before final polish

7

SKI INSTRUCTOR COURSES

Entry Qualifications, Examinations
Instructor Grading
Governing Bodies of Skiing

SKI INSTRUCTOR COURSES

The need for an examination and certification of ski instructors occurred in Britain during the period of skiing development as outlined in Chapter 1. In the interests of presenting to the winter tourist industry an overall standard of ski instruction, B.A.S.I. was appointed to undertake courses for instructors. These courses have been successfully organised from the inaugural training and certification meeting in 1963 and continue to expand in the content and number of candidates. In addition to the demands for uniform instruction on snow, the increased number of artificial ski slopes has brought about the need for special courses to standardise instruction in this important part of ski sport. For intending candidates an outline is given here of the entrance qualifications and the general organisation of these courses.

Candidate's entry qualifications

The first requirement of a candidate is the ability to ski to a certain standard. On snow courses this minimum requirement is to be able to ski good parallel turns on the piste. Should a candidate's performance be considered below this standard, the course organisers can refuse to give an examination test. In addition, it is useful to have a practical knowledge of general skiing and if possible, to have had some experience of elementary ski teaching. Possession of the elementary First-Aid Cert. is recommended. The minimum age qualifications are 16 years for Grade III and 18 years for Grades II and I. For artificial slope instructor courses, the candidate should be 18 years of age, have some teaching experience and ski to the basic parallel standard.

Course Syllabus

The daily programme of the course takes the form of outside practical skiing sessions and evening lectures. Trainers give perfectioning instruction to bring the personal performance of the candidate up to the high standard required of a ski instructor. Practical teaching sessions are given to familiarise the candidate with the methods of class handling and technique progression. In addition, advanced technique sessions are held in order to bring the candidate up to date with the latest technical developments.

The lecture and film programme covers all aspects of technique, equipment, first-aid and general mountain safety. The use of video-tape recording to analyse skiing performance and discussion forums further add to the varied coverage of all matters involved in the work of ski instruction.

Examination   A candidate is tested for technical skiing ability and teaching ability. The technical examination requires the candidate to demonstrate in finished form all the progression manoeuvres according to the standard of certification (the minimum standard is for smooth linked parallel turns). In addition the candidate has to make a free run over varied terrain. The teaching examination covers the candidate's class handling ability. Assessment marks are made on the choice of terrain, approach to class, manoeuvre explanation, demonstration, fault correction, exercise progression, class activity, audibility, position and general impression of the instructor. Verbal questions are also asked on all aspects of skiing. A written test is taken by Grade I instructors. The trainer completes individual report cards on class work and these are used in the overall assessment of the candidate.

British qualifications

Ski Party Leader

A week's course specially designed to meet the requirements of youth leaders, teachers and others who lead skiing groups. Good parallel skiing is required, ensuring that the candidate has a broad knowledge of the sport. Minimum age entry 21 years.

Artificial Ski Slope Instructor

This is the qualification required to teach basic ski manoeuvres on artificial ski slopes. Courses and tests are administered by the British Ski Federation, regional councils and by the Scottish National Ski Council. Full details of regional coaching schemes can be obtained from the head office addresses.

Grade III Assistant Ski Instructor

The first step towards a higher qualification in ski instruction. A high standard of personal performance is necessary and the candidate will be required to teach Parallel Turns and Short Swings.

Grade II Ski Instructor

The candidate must have passed the Grade III examination and have taught in a recognised ski school for at least one season. A very high skiing standard is required to obtain this qualification.

Grade I Teacher

This is the highest British instruction certificate requiring further ski school experience and having the Grade II qualification. A comprehensive written examination completes the high standard demanded for certification.

Trainer and Assessor

Grade I Ski Teachers may attend training for assessment to the Trainers' Registration List.

National Race Trainer

Candidates of suitable skiing experience attend a series of special courses concerning all aspects of racing and physical training.

THE ORGANISING BODIES OF SKIING

The British Association of Ski Instructors, Secretary,
Inverdruie, Aviemore, PH22 1QH, Inverness-shire. Tel. 0479-810407
> The Association is the official body for training and grading Ski Instructors throughout Great Britain. Has technical representation in Race Training and Artificial Slope Ski Instructors. Member of the International Ski Instructors' Association, representing UK at Interski Congresses.

The British Federation of Great Britain,
118 Eaton Square, London SW1. Tel. 01-235-8227
> The senior representative of British skiing, and consti-tuent member of the International Ski Federation — F.I.S. Undertakes the training and racing arrange-ments for British competitors in Alpine and Nordic events. Administers tests and coaching schemes for artificial slopes, and ASSI examinations. Liases with regional councils and the Sports Council.

Scottish National Ski Council,
110A Maxwell Avenue, Bearsden, Glasgow, G61. Tel. 041-943-0760.
> Administers all matters concerned with clubs, racing, Ski Party Leaders and general promotion of skiing in Scotland.

English Ski Council, Library Buildings, The Precinct,
Halesowen, West Midlands.

Ski Council of Wales.

Regional Ski Associations
> These Councils and Associations organise coaching schemes and other relevant skiing matters that are concerned with their respective areas.

International Ski Instructors' Association
> Consists of representatives from all national ski in-struction organisations. Organises Interski Congress periodically, to review developments in ski technique and teaching methods.

Federation Internationale de Ski (F.I.S.)
> The international controlling body for all skiing matters.

Governing Bodies of Skiing

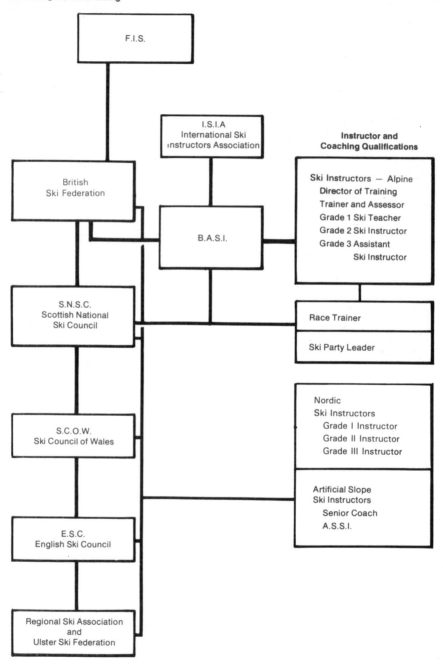

F.I.S.

I.S.I.A
International Ski
Instructors Association

**Instructor and
Coaching Qualifications**

British
Ski Federation

B.A.S.I.

Ski Instructors — Alpine
Director of Training
Trainer and Assessor
Grade 1 Ski Teacher
Grade 2 Ski Instructor
Grade 3 Assistant
Ski Instructor

S.N.S.C.
Scottish National
Ski Council

Race Trainer

Ski Party Leader

S.C.O.W.
Ski Council of Wales

Nordic
Ski Instructors
Grade I Instructor
Grade II Instructor
Grade III Instructor

Artificial Slope
Ski Instructors
Senior Coach
A.S.S.I.

E.S.C.
English Ski Council

Regional Ski Association
and
Ulster Ski Federation

GLOSSARY OF SKIING TERMS

Angulation
The outward leaning of the body from the slope, or to the outside of a turn. Knees and hips are pressed into the slope or inside of the turn.

Anticipation
Turning of the body in advance of turning the skis in the same direction — pre-twisting — used with stick plant at the turn preparation phase.

Avalement
French ski manoeuvre using folded legs to absorb bumpy terrain.

Backward Lean
Leaning back to place the centre of gravity behind the centre of the feet.

Basic Stance
Comfortably flexed body position over the skis while sliding, without exaggerated twisting or angulation of the upper body.

Basic Swing
Derived from 'Grundschwung' — uses snowplough start and parallel swing finish.

Camber
Curved shape of ski along the sole from tip to heel.

Carving
Turning or steering the ski or skis, with the minimum of sideslip using reverse camber edge-carve effect from the skis.

Change of lead
Changing from one ski leading to the opposite ski leading.

Check
A pronounced edge-setting of the skis into the snow, used to brake or provide a platform from which to initiate a turn.

Compression
Lowering of body by folding of legs to keep constant pressure on the skis. Used to compensate for skis turning over bumpy terrain.

Controlling Phase
That part of a turning arc that has to be controlled or steered.

Counter
A turning motion in one direction that results a turning movement in the opposite direction.

Downmotion
Lowering of the body by bending at the hips, knees and ankles — as in downsinking movement.

Edge-set
Angular setting of the ski soles and edges into the snow.

Fall-line
The line of least resistance down a slope.

Flatten
Reducing the amount of edge-set to flatten the skis relative to the snow surface.

Forward Lean
Position leaning forward to place the centre of gravity in front of the centre of the feet.

Garlands	Linked exercise movements traversing across the slope.
Initiation Phase	The moment the skis are displaced into the turning direction.
Inner Ski	The inside ski of a turn.
Inside Edge	The ski edge towards the inside of the turn.
Lateral Displacement	Sliding of the skis, or pivotting, to displace the skis sideways.
Natural Stance	As for Basic Stance — a natural comfortable position for skiing.
Open Stance	Skiing stance with the feet and skis open, to widen the balance platform.
Outside Edge	The outer edge of the ski to the outside of the turn.
Outer ski	The outside ski of the turn.
Ploughing	Stemming of both skis at an angle from the tips.
Preparation Phase	The movements made to prepare for initiating the turn.
Rebound	The reaction from an edge-set and leg movement, to unweight the skis.
Retraction	Drawing up of the legs under the body by a folding action.
Rotation	Rotational turning movement of the body in the ski turn direction.
Side-slip	Releasing edge-set to allow the skis to slip laterally.
Steering	Pressure applied to the forward part of the skis to steer round the turn.
Stemming	Displacing the skis at an angle to one another from the tips.
Stick Plant	Placing of the ski stick into the snow as an aid to turning movements. Also termed Pole Plant.
Swing	Curve side-slip or turning arc with skis parallel.
Teaching Method or Plan	The method by which ski technique is taught to a student.
Technique	The technical detailed description of a skiing manoeuvre.
Traverse	Crossing a slope at an angle to the fall-line.
Turn	Changing direction while skiing.
Unweighting	Reducing the weight pressure on the skis by body movements to initiate a turning manoeuvre.
Upmotion	Extending of the legs and body to unweight the skis.

Upper/Lower Ski	Relative position of skis to the snow slope.
Wedeln	Continuous smooth turns made in quick succession without excessive edge-set.
Wedging	Stemming out the skis from the tips, as in Ploughing.
Weight Transfer	Changing the weight pressure from one ski to the other.
Wellen	Austrian technique for skiing moguls using bending and stretching of the legs.

BIBLIOGRAPHY

Ski Technique —

The Official American Ski Technique — P.S.I.A.Inc., Denver, Colo., U.S.A.

Osterreichischer Schilehrplan — O.B. Otto Muller Verlag, Salzburg, Austria.

Skilehrplan — Deutscher V.f.s. BLV Verlag, Muchen, W. Germany.

Ski in der Schweiz — Schweizer Skischulverband, Berne, Switzerland.

Canadian Ski School Manual — Canadian Ski Instructors' Alliance, Montreal, Quebec, Canada.

French Ski Teaching Handbook — Ecoles du Ski Francais, Paris.

Italian Ski Manual — Fed. I. Sport Invernali (Ski School), Milan.

Biomechanics Manual — P.S.I.A.Inc., Seattle, U.S.A.

Ski the New French Way — Joubert & Vuarnet, Kaye and Ward, London.

How the Racers Ski — Waren Witherell, W. W. Norton & Co., New York.

We Learned to Ski — Sunday Times, Collins, London.

Ski Coaching in Scotland — SNSC, Bearsden, Glasgow.

Coaching Scheme Booklet — English Ski Council, NSFGB, London.

Safety —

A.B.C. of Avalanche Safety — E. R. La Chapelle, Outdoor Sports Industries Inc., Denver, U.S.A.

Avalanche Enigma — Colin Fraser, Murray, London.

Snow Avalanches — U.S. Dept. of Agriculture Handbook, No. 194, Washington.

Mountain Leadership — E. Langmuir, Scottish Sports Council, Edinburgh.

Mountaineering — Manual — D. Roscoe, Faber, London.

Safety on Mountains Pamphlet — C.C.P.R., Sports Council, London.

Snow Structure, Ski Fields, G. Seligman, Jos. Adam, Brussels.

Mountain Rescue Handbook — H. McInnes, Mountain Rescue Committee.

First-Aid Manual — St. Andrew's Ambulance Association and British Red Cross Society.

NOTES

NOTES

NOTES

NOTES

ISBN 0 904212 00 9

HARLEY & COX (PRINTERS) LTD.
4 SHAFTESBURY ROAD
DUNDEE DD2 1UL